The Miracle of
INSTANT MEMORY POWER

The Miracle of
INSTANT MEMORY POWER

by
David V. Lewis

Parker Publishing Company, Inc.
West Nyack, New York

© 1973, by

PARKER PUBLISHING COMPANY, INC.

West Nyack, N.Y.

All rights reserved. No part of this book may be reproduced in any form or by any means, without permission in writing from the publisher.

Library of Congress Cataloging in Publication Data

Lewis, Dave.
 The miracle of instant memory power.

 1. Mnemonics.   I. Title.
BF385.L56   153.1'4   72-11515
ISBN 0-13-585273-0

Printed in the United States of America

How This Book Can Help Change Your Life

You can improve your memory virtually overnight—even if it's an extremely "bad one"—by using the techniques discussed in this book.

Once mastered, these proven techniques will provide you with a powerful memory—a memory that will enable you to retain facts instantly and efficiently.

In a short while, you'll find yourself confidently meeting and remembering the names of a roomful of people. You'll be able to recall long lists of disconnected facts, important dates, and speeches. If you like, you can even perform impressive parlor feats like remembering a current magazine or deck of cards.

If you're one who professes to have a "poor memory" (and who hasn't at one time or another?), you'll be amazed at the seemingly miraculous manner in which you are able to flash facts, instantly, to your memory. There's no prolonged meditation or endless mind-searching involved. You simply use these proven techniques to lock facts in your memory like a vise, instantly.

You'll be pleasantly surprised at how quickly and thoroughly you can retain an almost infinite variety of facts. Again, if you've long considered your memory a weak link in your mental makeup, you'll be amazed at the miracle-like transformation after you've mastered these principles. That's what I mean by "miracle"—the astonishing improvement you can work in your own life if you conscientiously apply these principles of memory development.

You'll not only learn to use these powerful techniques to master some of the more difficult areas of memory, like names and faces, but also you'll learn how to:

* Remember more of what you hear and read.
* Use your native intelligence more effectively.
* Observe more accurately.
* Use your senses to greater advantage.
* Use visualization and association with far greater efficiency.
* Use spaced learning, repetition, recitation, and a host of other sound psychological learning methods.

In a very short while, you'll have the confident, positive attitude characteristic of the person who has developed all-around instant memory power.

Rewards for the person who can develop instant memory power can mount beyond expectations.

You can improve your social and business stature by constantly sharpening your ability to remember names and faces—one of the greatest personal assets you can develop. You can make a lasting impression by being able to make an extemporaneous speech without referring to copious notes. Or you can shine at the business conference by coming up with that hard-to-remember fact that no one can seem to recall.

Indeed, you'll find instant memory power to be one of the greatest social and business assets you can possess.

David V. Lewis

CONTENTS

How This Book Can Help Change Your Life 5

CHAPTER 1   Shooting for a Money-Making Instant Memory . 13
Basic Tools for an Outstanding Memory (14)
The Physiology of Memory (15)
Memory and Age (16)
Types of Memory (18)
Using Your Native Talent (19)

CHAPTER 2   How a Positive Attitude Can Help Build
Instant Memory Power 21
Finding Reasons for Remembering (22)
Setting Up Memory Goals (23)
The Right Mental Approach (24)
How Interest Aids Memory (25)
Overcoming Negative Attitudes (26)
The Role of Intention (27)

CHAPTER 3   Nine Ways to Concentrate Better with
Instant Memory Power. 29
Eliminating Distractions (30)
Shelving Your Problems (30)
Getting Set to Listen (31)
Reading Rapidly (32)
Scheduling Your Time (32)
Working Rapidly (33)
Breaking the Job Down (33)

CHAPTER 3	Nine Ways to Concentrate Better with Instant Memory Power (Cont'd.)

Taking Action (34)
Exercising Your Mind (35)

CHAPTER 4	Using Your Senses to Create Instant Memory Storage	37

Writing It Down (37)
Using All Your Senses (38)
Combining Senses (39)
How Note-Taking Helps (40)
How Reciting Helps (41)
Sharpening Your Listening Skill (42)
Tips for Effective Listening (43)
Tips for Instant Memory Power Observation (45)

CHAPTER 5	Making Your Mind Work Like a Computer with Instant Memory Power	47

The Psychology of Remembering (48)
Principles of Association (50)
How Your Subconscious Uses Association (51)
The Process of Visualization (53)
How Visualization Helps (54)
Photographic Memory (54)
Combining Visualizing and Associating (56)
An Experiment You Can Perform (56)

CHAPTER 6	Increasing Mental Efficiency with Instant Memory Power	59

How We Forget (60)
Overlearning for Memorizing (61)
How to Memorize Speeches and Reports (62)
How Reminiscence Works (63)
The Best Time to Memorize (64)
Rules for Effective Studying (64)
Using Self-Rewards (66)

CHAPTER 7	Using Instant Memory Power Techniques to Read Better and Retain More	69

Increasing Your Reading Ability (69)

Contents

CHAPTER 7 Using Instant Memory Power Techniques to
Read Better and Retain More (Cont'd.)
Reading at an Appropriate Speed (70)
How Skimming Can Improve Reading (71)
When to Read Slowly (72)
Reciting What You Have Read (74)
The Goal of Comprehension (74)
Putting Reading Principles to Work (76)

CHAPTER 8 Adding to Your Instant Memory Power Through
Mnemonics—Shorthand of the Mind (for Facts
and Dates).................................85
The "Shorthand" Memory Alphabet (86)
Forming Memorable Key Words (87)
Remembering Sales Features (88)
Learning Numbers in "Parts" (91)
Remembering Phone Numbers (92)
Remembering Code Numbers (93)

CHAPTER 9 Doubling Your Instant Memory Power with
an Alternate Channel..................... 97
Using Logical Extension (97)
Switching Memory Channels (98)
Remembering a List of Regulations (99)
Remembering Playing Cards (102)

CHAPTER 10 Using Instant Memory Power to Create a
Mental Calendar........................105
Months as Pictures (105)
Remembering Earlier Historic Dates (107)
Remembering the Day of the Month (108)
Remembering a Busy Schedule (110)
Speaking Without Notes (113)

CHAPTER 11 Using Instant Memory Power to Master
Hard-to-Recall Facts 115
Secretarial Spelling Crutches (116)
Learning Words by Association (117)
"Hard" Numbers Made Easy (118)
Developing Your "Miscellaneous Memory" (119)

CHAPTER 11 Using Instant Memory Power to Master
            Hard-to-Recall Facts (Cont'd.)
    Using an Acrostic for a Crutch (119)
    Remembering the Presidents (121)

CHAPTER 12 Using Instant Memory Power to Remember
            Names—Sure-Fire Shortcut to Success 125
    Psychology of Name-Remembering (126)
    Using Proper Mental Set (127)
    Selecting an Outstanding Feature (128)
    Getting the Name Right (131)
    How to Remember First Names (133)
    Tying in with an Outstanding Feature (140)
    Finding Other Areas of Association (144)
    Testing Yourself on Names (150)
    Starting Your Name Notebook (199)

The Miracle of
INSTANT MEMORY POWER

Shooting for a Money-Making Instant Memory

1

It's virtually impossible to think of a single mental act in which memory does not play a key role.

In making a routine decision, for example, an executive usually considers a number of things. What are the facts involved? How will the decision affect his company?... His people? Has the idea worked—or failed—elsewhere? What are the precedents? These and perhaps scores of other ideas and impressions must be dredged from memory, often within seconds. Most executives make many such decisions daily, based on data furnished by the recall mechanism.

The business and professional man's memory is further challenged in a host of workaday situations. He must carry around, on the tip of his memory, an awesome array of facts: names and faces, important dates, statistics, appointments, and key points in company contracts, among other things. And for good measure, how about birthdays and anniversaries?

Even in leisure hours, memory must perform in yeoman fashion. When playing a seven iron into a strong wind, precisely how should he play the ball? He must fall back on his "muscle memory" to furnish the answer. If he's a duffer, all the worse; he can recall only bogeys.

Basic Tools for an Outstanding Memory

How about your memory? Does it instantly "flash" you names and facts? Does it usually furnish the right name and the appropriate fact? Or does it routinely fail you in crucial situations, or take many long minutes to "come up with" answers?

The speed and efficiency of your memory depend, to a degree, on your mental makeup. A fortunate few are blessed with a seemingly natural ability to retain a great deal of what they see and hear. Conversely, there are those—a relative handful—who are hampered by low mentality and poor memory.

But most fall somewhere in between these two extremes. There simply isn't a great deal of difference in the average person's *ability* to remember, though differences in performance are often apparent. The average person will usually admit that his memory is "good enough to get by on," but he will scoff at the notion that he carries within himself all the basic tools needed for a truly quick, outstanding memory. To possess such power seems miraculous—but the average person usually has these requirements. In a nutshell, they include: average intelligence; strong desire and motivation; positive attitude; well-developed senses; and a willingness to use proven techniques systematically in learning situations.

That's what this book is all about—*training* yourself to use these proven techniques and methods in a routine fashion, to remember the things you consider relevant to your life-style. Why get along with a mediocre memory when, with a little extra effort—every day—you can develop genuine "instant memory" power?

What's to be gained from developing instant memory power? Here's what Theodore Ynetma, erstwhile vice-president of Ford Motor Company, had to say: "Many a man, by memory, has gone far beyond his competitor, who in analytical power, outranked him."

Shooting for a Money-Making Instant Memory 15

Clearly, the person who can use his instant memory power to come up routinely with the right answer gets the promotion: The person who can amaze others with his ability to remember names and faces wins friends and influences almost everyone. The man who can speak off-the-cuff, without using bulky notes, gains the respect of his fellowmen. In short, the man with the outstanding memory—with genuine instant memory power—is destined to get ahead.

Before getting down to brass tacks about practical memory techniques, let's look briefly into the nature of this fascinating thing we call memory. What is it and how does it "take place"?

The Physiology of Memory

Modern physiologists estimate that the human brain is composed of more than 10 billion neurons or cells. Remembering—and other mental processes—causes the neurons to discharge an electrical current. When we remember, a sort of neuron chain is formed in the brain tissue; the impression is "tattooed" onto the cerebral cortex. Since the neurons may be a part of a number of separate patterns, the human brain's capacity to learn and remember would appear almost limitless.

These cells of gray matter seem to connect in a vast network that is complex beyond human imagination. It is probably so comprehensive that the whole cortex can be thought of as one great unit of integrated activity. And if it is to be considered a machine, it must be thought of as the most complicated machine in existence.

Because of the mind's ability to retain vast amounts of information and impressions, it is often likened to a computer. But how would a human mind stack up against the electronic marvel? Perhaps Y. Saprina, author of *Cybernetics Within Us* (Wilshire Book Company, Hollywood, California) gives some insight. A computer, he says, stores or memorizes a half-million pages of printed matter, or over 2,000 200-page books. Nerve fibers, he concludes, have an information-carrying capability of 140,000 bits of information in one second. This means theoretically the brain is capable of receiving 140,000 bits of information in a single second. Over an average life span of 70 years, he says, the storage capacity of the human brain turns out to be a million times greater than that of most information-storage machines.

Man further has it all over the computer in that he can use judgment; the machine can remember only what man feeds into it. But, before you begin to feel too superior, consider that a computer, once it receives information—say, a name—never forgets it. How many names have you forgotten lately?

Memory and Age

The ability of the mind to link or associate facts and ideas in this vast cranial network will be discussed more fully in the chapter on association. Briefly, however, let's explore the popular belief that memory begins to misfire more frequently after, say, 40. Many middle-aged executives feel they're about to go over the hill, intellectually speaking, simply because a memory trace fades here and there. But there's considerable evidence to the contrary. This evidence suggests strongly that the person who develops instant memory power may actually hit his mental peak in these "later" years! Here, for example, is what modern gerontology (study of age) says about it.

Admittedly, a person's physical reflexes slow somewhat as he grows older. Additionally, some diseases like goiter, anemia, blood-vessel disorders, and hardening of the brain arteries—to name the more serious ones—are linked with memory impairment. Aside from such ailments, however, gerontologists say there's no positive proof that mental "deficiency" comes at any certain age, except perhaps in extreme age.

Some interesting facts about the American executive's mental makeup have been revealed by Dr. Ward C. Halstead, professor of psychology and director of medical psychology at the University of Chicago. In an effort to check for brain deterioration in "aging" executives, he developed a battery of tests to measure such factors as judgment, perception, and memory power. Routine checkups of selected men pointed out that four of five executives up to age 50 functioned as well mentally as most 25-year-old junior executives.

Shooting for a Money-Making Instant Memory

Beyond 50, he found, deterioration was slightly greater, with most breakdowns taking place in the 60s and 70s. Significantly, the drop in mental efficiency was so slight that it made no appreciable difference in performance. "The added experience," he said, "more than overcame the slight loss of brainpower in most cases." His conclusion: the brain does not necessarily age as tissues of the body do. One person may be "old" mentally at 50; another may be mentally productive and alert at 70 and beyond. ("Brainpower Tests Rate Executives," *Nation's Business,* Feb. 1958, The Chamber of Commerce of the United States.)

The type of work a person does may be a big factor in determining continued mental alertness. In one experiment, 12 students who had taken the Army's Alpha Test (one of the first tests to measure mental ability) in World War I, were located and retested. Each scored higher than in the original series. The survey revealed that most of these former collegians had remained mentally alert in various fields since graduation. The results could, and probably would have been different if the group had not been doing basically mental-type work in the intervening years.

At Columbia University, Dr. Irving Lodge found that students up to 70 and above could learn Russian and shorthand as easily as their younger classmates could. Stronger motivation and higher interest were given as partial reasons for this apparently successful effort to bridge the mental age gap.

From appearances, then, the more mature people who remain mentally active have several things going for them in a learning situation. Indeed, development of the nervous system may be progressive in this respect. Some psychologists, like Walter B. Pillsbury of the University of Michigan, claim that capacity for remembering, in some instances, increases with age. "It's possible," he said, "that an increase in knowledge in divergent fields makes attention more certain... and perhaps more association bonds are formed to receive new material and make association in new directions." In other words, the more you know, the easier it is to tie in new facts and concepts. "Firmness and holding to task," he concluded, "often increase with years and can result in increased memory efficiency in some cases."

Some consider varied interests and sustained mental involvement as the answer to memory efficiency in "senior citizens." Oliver Wendell Holmes, for example, read avidly through his 93rd year to "improve my mind." France's venerable statesman, Clemenceau, put it this way: "The secret is simple ... never let your brain grow inactive, and you will keep young forever." Emerson added: "We do not count a man's years until he has nothing else to count."

Mental alacrity is also linked closely with physical fitness, regardless of age. "Fatigue plays an important part in loss of memory," says Dr. Wadlemar Schweisheimer, "and plenty of sleep and rest can go a long way to restore it. Many a youthful employee whose forgetfulness keeps both his boss and his co-workers on pins and needles would have a far better memory were he to give himself more time to sleep and rest his brain."

Types of Memory

Philosophical aspects of memory aside, the question persists: Can you, on a practical basis, actually *improve* your memory? Most so-called memory experts contend memory is "like a muscle"—exercise it, and it will grow. Many psychologists, on the other hand, are quick to point out that a person's memory capability is much like his intelligence quotient. It's a natural capability which can't be improved upon materially. Put in perspective, both points of view have merit. Here's why.

Memory appears, in a great number of cases, to be a specific talent. For example, the technique you'll use to recall names can't be used with any degree of success to remember, say, a speech. But then, neither can the methods used to remember the speech— namely, the basic "laws" of learning—be used to recall the names of a group of people. Thus the dilemma. And thus the need for memory techniques to match the situation.

In learning the speech, you are called on to remember a logical body of ideas with a central theme or purpose. You can, by and large, use the same learning techniques here that you would use in trying to remember any logical body of information.

Shooting for a Money-Making Instant Memory

But recalling a group of names poses a different—and to many, a far more formidable—problem. The names are almost always totally illogical in nature. They simply have no inherent meaning. Even an "easy" name like Smith can be a stickler, since there's no real *reason* for him to have the name. Repeating the name will help, but in many cases repetition alone won't pin the name down for you. This is where the person with instant memory power shifts gears mentally. Since he can't use a logical approach, he settles for a mnemonic or artificial technique.

The mnemonic technique, then, can be justified as the only "logical" way to remember not only names, but other abstract and "meaningless" things, such as disconnected facts, numbers, and random bits of information that make little or no sense in themselves. It can be a powerful weapon, as demonstrated by the more proficient memory experts. Some can use this highly developed mnemonic technique to "memorize" entire magazines, or names of a large roomful of people.

While a mnemonic approach can work wonders for you in these difficult areas of memory, it obviously is not a cure-all. Here's where the man who builds an "instant memory" power puts things in perspective. He learns first to develop efficient learning habits, the basis for his instant memory power. Then he learns to master mnemonic techniques which will make him a whiz at remembering abstract things like names and numbers. Once he's done this, he's on his way to instant memory power.

With practice, you'll be able to use these mnemonic techniques to help you remember names, numbers, and disconnected facts more successfully. The more you practice (exercise, if you will), the more efficient your memory will become in these highly abstract areas—but only in these areas. So, to this extent, you can improve your memory by *exercising a technique.*

Using Your Native Talent

The psychologist, of course, has some scientific basis for his memory theory. Very likely, we are born with a certain memory prowess, just as we come equipped with varying degrees of intelligence. But how we use our native intelligence—and memory—is something else. While it's probably true that you can't improve upon your natural endowment, you can undoubtedly improve the methods used to learn and recall. In this sense, you may be able to improve your memory, sometimes dramatically, by improving the manner in which you acquire information.

"What is needed," says Dr. Donald A. Laird, a well-known psychologist, "is not a stronger memory, but better management of the memory." In this sense, he says, memory improvement should be aimed at improving your memory efficiency so that it will serve as an aid to overall mental activity.

Technically, memory involves three basic steps: acquiring, retaining, and, finally, recalling. We can improve memory to the extent that we can stimulate greater efficiency in any of these areas. Making up your mind to become more mentally efficient is the first step toward "instant memory" power.

How a Positive Attitude Can Help Build Instant Memory Power 2

Back in the heyday of television quiz shows, Joyce Brothers literally breezed through "The $64,000 Question" by reciting a host of little-known facts about boxing. Most of the questions would have stumped most veteran sportswriters.

Many viewers, no doubt, wondered if things were on the level. Did this attractive blonde, a lecturer in psychology at Hunter College, actually know this much about the manly business of boxing? Had she really stashed away this wealth of peripheral detail over the years? The answer, of course, was no. Joyce Brothers got most of her information straight from *The Encyclopedia of Boxing,* and here's how she did it:

"I spent five intensive weeks learning every nook and cranny of that huge book. I learned of fights I had no idea had taken place. I accumulated facts about the history of the fight game that made me more and more fascinated as I went along. These were, of course, facts that are ordinarily not important to the average boxing fan. But I realized if I wanted to go on the program and win the $64,000 prize, I had to have a knowledge that was going to be greater. Not only did I study *The Encyclopedia of Boxing,* but also I read every other book and magazine article about the subject I could lay my hands on." *(10 Days to a Successful Memory,* Prentice-Hall, 1957).

Amazingly, Joyce Brothers admitted to having little or no interest in boxing before her prolonged cramming session. She acquired a passing interest from her medical-student husband, a genuine fight fan. But it wasn't until they were expecting a baby that she developed serious interest. She decided to quit teaching so she could stay home with her children; on the other hand, she wanted her husband to continue his studies. To do both would require more money. This dilemma prompted her to become an "instant" boxing expert. As a result, she won a small fortune.

Certainly, Dr. Brothers is a highly intelligent person with a strong memory. But it's doubtful that even a person of her acumen could have mastered *The Encyclopedia of Boxing* without the strongest of motives. Her story illustrates one of the fundamental "rules" of memory. *Generally speaking, the stronger the motive or reason for remembering, the more efficiently the memory functions.* Without the $64,000 jackpot as a goal, would Joyce Brothers have retained those seemingly insignificant details? Probably not.

Finding Reasons for Remembering

One of the first steps, then, in developing an instant memory power is to find strong *reasons* for remembering.

For example, it's easy to visualize the benefits of an instant memory power on the job. You can reel off important facts and figures about your products, quote interesting facts about your company, recall details of business conferences. Or, you might use your instant memory power to give an off-the-cuff talk or report. If your instant memory power had no other virtue than making you competent at remembering names and faces, it would be worth the effort. Super-salesmen say a quick, powerful memory is one of their greatest assets. The rewards can be manifold: more pay, a better job, a strong sense of attainment, and a confident and positive personality. It's up to you to find memory motives to fit your life-style—and when you do, you're on your way.

Setting Up Memory Goals

Some psychologists say the best way to establish firm motives is to set up specific, on-going goals that relate directly to your needs. Dr. Bluma Zeigarnik of the University of Berlin tested to see what happened when students didn't finish tasks or goals they had started. Most students remembered unfinished chores roughly 50% better than similar ones that they finished without interruption. Why did they remember unfinished assignments better? Perhaps because of the tension theory postulated by Kurt Lewin, another prominent German psychologist. Lewin felt that a person normally has a strong urge to complete any task that he has set for himself. Merely starting toward the goal, he says, sets off a sort of inner tension, and this condition is not "satisfied" until the task is finished—the goal is reached. Proof of the theory seems to lie in the oft-repeated expression, "I won't be able to do a thing until I finish this job."

The more personal and specific your goals, the better. But the beauty of the theory is, these goals need not relate to memory *per se*. As an executive, for example, you might set a personal goal of establishing a stronger communications program in your organization. This will require extensive research, including firsthand inspection of some model organizations. During this time, you will gather volumes of data, with an eye to making a convincing case in your final written report. You will, of course, keep notes. When the time comes to state your case, your memory will probably work wonders for you. You will recall many facts and impressions, offhand. Or, being unable to do this, you will remember precisely where to get the information. Such is the way memory works for the goal-oriented. Reading and investigating with a particular purpose in mind gives your memory a specific target to aim for.

This helps facts and impressions to jell in a more meaningful way in your mind.

Finding a motive and setting appropriate, realistic goals is a seemingly logical initial step in any learning situation. Realistic motives, like more pay, rapid promotion, and strong personality, go hand-in-glove with an instant memory.

The Right Mental Approach

Taking this action leads to three other important preliminary steps: showing proper interest, intending to remember, and developing a more positive mental approach. All these factors—motive, interest, intent, and positive approach—form what psychologists call mental set or attitude. They are responsible for putting you in the "right frame of mind" for remembering important things.

Famed educational psychologist, Robert S. Woodworth, stressed the importance of mental set, claiming it influences not only how you "see" something, but how well you remember it. "Mental set," he said, "is a highly selective and active process that favors some responses and prevents others." Woodworth further defined "set" as *preparatory* (a condition in which a person readies himself for a specific response, such as getting ready for a race) or *continuing* (which involves virtually a perpetual state of readiness). A salesman who wants to remember the name of every prospective customer, for example, should be more or less permanently prepared to use a technique to remember them.

The other facets of mental set—interest, intent, and positive mental outlook—must be practiced routinely in developing your instant memory power.

Interest is usually a by-product of proper motivation and goal-striving. Some educators go so far as to say that interest is the single most important factor in learning or remembering. You've known the relative futility of trying to remember when you have had little interest in the subject. The restless schoolboy is often a case in point. He's a "dunce" in the classroom, but a veritable wizard when it comes to spouting batting averages or intricate football formations.

How Interest Aids Memory

Extreme interest often results in memory performance bordering on the fantastic. Arturo Toscanini, the great Italian conductor, memorized all of the major symphonic and operatic scores. When he was only 19, he was called on at the last minute to lead a performance of *Aida*. He accepted the challenge and performed flawlessly, strictly from memory. Winston Churchill, historians say, could often commit lengthy political talks to memory in as few as a couple of readings—a really quick "learn." George C. Marshall, United States Chief of Staff in World War II, was allegedly a master of memory at a press conference. So the story goes, he could field dozens of questions, then answer the queries in succession without further reference to the question or the reporter. Napoleon, history tells us, was a genius at remembering battles and even the names of rear-rank soldiers.

None of these famous men was regarded as scholarly. In truth, each had a superior memory capability in the area of his greatest interest. From his ninth year, Toscanini's life evolved around music. Marshall was completely dedicated to the military, as was Napoleon. And Churchill was an absolute genius at remembering anything of significance, even though, according to his valet, he was forever forgetting where he put his eyeglasses and false teeth.

Interest, then, is a vital ingredient in evolving the proper attitude or "set" for your instant memory. Joyce Brothers, you'll recall, had little or no interest in boxing until she was strongly motivated. Then her interest skyrocketed. Make a "memory check." You'll probably find your memory works well where you have sufficient interest, perhaps not so well in other areas. This exercise should pinpoint areas in which you need to improve most. If you're interested enough and willing to pay the price for an instant memory power, you probably can become a Toscanini or Churchill in your own field.

Overcoming Negative Attitudes

The next step in creating proper mental set is to develop a more positive mental attitude. "I've got a horrible memory"; "I just can't remember names"; "Don't ask me if it happened over 10 minutes ago—I've forgotten"; "My memory is like a sieve"—these and countless other utterances are used so frequently by so many that they have become memory clichés. If you're not guilty, consider yourself the exception. Many of us have developed strong negative attitudes toward our memory because of the very nature of the function. Even the more efficient forget frequently, although many of the things forgotten are probably sloughed off mentally as not being relevant to one's life-style.

There is, on the other hand, considerable justification for being downright proud of your memory. It houses more facts, figures, ideas, and impressions than a computer stores. The fact that you can recall addresses, telephone numbers, service serial numbers, childhood experiences, stock-market quotations, abstract ideas, and a limitless list of things at any one moment, certainly attests to the super-efficiency of this cerebral function. And in your work, it's an absolute workhorse.

The point is, no person is perfect in the memory department, nor would he really want to be. But the athlete who enters the fray thinking he will lose, frequently does. Common sense tells him that he can't win every race, but the successful athlete thinks he is *capable* of doing so.

Little negatives ("I just can't remember") soon blossom into full-grown negative attitudes, according to Dr. Norman Vincent Peale, the country's foremost advocate of positive thinking. "It is important," he says, "to eliminate from conversations all negative ideas, for they tend to produce tension and annoyance inwardly."

A positive approach of more recent vintage is taken by Dr. Maxwell Maltz, plastic surgeon and author of *Psycho-Cybernetics*

(Prentice-Hall, Inc., Englewood Cliffs, N.J.). Dr. Maltz likens the subconscious mind and nervous system to a "servo-mechanism," like the one that guides a missile to its target. Fed erroneous information, the "servo-mechanism" will make the missile veer from course. Similarly, the individual's subconscious, fed negative thoughts over a period of years, will steer the memory along false paths. There is a tendency, Dr. Maltz asserts, for you to try to live up to the impression of yourself created in your "servo-mechanism." In other words, if you tell yourself that you can't remember names, sure enough . . . you probably can't.

The Role of Intention

Intending to remember can often make the difference between remembering quite well or not at all. Numerous psychological experiments have shown that a person generally retains information for just about the period of time he "intends" to retain it. If, for example, you are trying to remember a report that you must give a week hence, there is a good chance you will retain the information quite well up to that time, then forget an appreciable amount of the material shortly thereafter. On the other hand, many of us have the audacity to fault our own memory, even though we had no *intention* of remembering at all. Think back over, say, to the last ten or 15 people to whom you were introduced. How many of their names can you recall? In retrospect, how many of the names did you really *intend* to recall in the first place? If you did not truthfully intend to remember and make an active effort to do so, it is more your mental set at fault than your memory.

These, then, are the steps to take in developing your all-important mental set or attitude toward an instant memory power.

Find the strongest possible memory motive and set on-going goals which will help you fulfill this motive.

Routinely show interest in that which you want to remember, emphasizing areas in which you do not have a naturally high interest level.

Assume a more positive mental attitude in all matters of memory.

And generally intend to remember.

The approach should be habitual, done consciously at first, then subconsciously as the pattern becomes an integral part of your reaction to any memory situation.

Your mental set influences the way you see things, and to a large degree, whether you remember them. Also, it is the starting point for developing your instant memory power.

3
Nine Ways to Concentrate Better with Instant Memory Power

Ben Hogan, one of golfdom's greatest, retired a few years ago because of "age" and "my inability to concentrate on my game."

Ability to concentrate? Isn't this the stock-in-trade of the scholarly ilk—doctors, lawyers, historians?

It is, but not exclusively. Psychologists tell us now that the ability to concentrate (pay close mental attention to one activity to the exclusion of others) is important in just about any pursuit. Samuel Johnson summed up the role of concentration in memory when he said, "The art of memory is the art of attention." There's probably not much difference in the average person's *ability* to concentrate. There is, however, frequently a big gap in *capability,* due mainly to the manner in which the more efficient go about this cerebral activity.

If you lack the ability to concentrate well, you may find solace in the belief that this is a God-given talent of the chosen. Unfortunately, many people do believe this, and so deprive themselves of what is probably the most important attribute of an efficient memory—the ability to focus attention.

You must, in effect, train yourself in a routine manner to pay close attention in every learning situation, then you will be on your way to that coveted instant memory. Actually, how well you do concentrate probably depends as much on your mental habits as it does on your intellect. Here are some of the methods suggested by leading psychologists for closer concentration:

1. *Eliminating distractions.* In World War II, aircraft executives found that production increased sharply and safety records improved when sweater girls were barred from the assembly line.

An office manager of a big insurance company discovered that placing extra-thick pads under typewriters cut down the high noise factor in his office. Result: more efficient typists and executives.

A promising writer said he made great progress for the first time last year. But only after he had summoned up enough will power to turn off the television set.

All of these things—the sweater girls, noisy typewriters, and the television set—were distractions. They kept people from paying attention to their work. Like many external distractions, they could be eliminated simply by shutting them out.

Some methods are subtler. For example, the employees of a small factory at first got a big kick out of the many THINK signs the "old man" had placed around the plant. But as it turned out, the boss knew what he was doing. "I find," he said, "that when people see enough of these signs, they finally get the idea that people really are thinking. They realize that loud talk and concentration don't go together, so they keep conversation down."

2. *Shelving your problems.* Inner distractions are infinitely more mysterious. Most of the time we don't know where they come from or why? They may be perfunctory in nature, like the sudden thought of an undone chore. Or, as is often the case, they are

serious, like gnawing anxiety over health or financial problems.

A lady fashion editor, admittedly slightly neurotic, used to have a hard time "keeping my head in the game." But not since she learned to keep a "box score" of her problems. When she caught her mind wandering, she would ask herself, "Now just what caused me to lose my chain of thought?"

"I would jot down my answers in the back of my memo pad. Then at the end of the week, I'd analyze the answers. It usually didn't take a psychiatrist to tell me what my problem was."

"Discovering the problem," she adds, "was often the solution itself. But if the problem couldn't be solved right away, I just put it on the shelf. Then I'd have a go at it later."

3. *Getting set to listen.* Many times, we fail to listen to a speaker simply because we aren't *ready* to pay attention. As mentioned earlier, this state of readiness is a *mental set*. It means that to pay full attention, you must get ready, both physically and mentally, to receive an idea or impression.

There probably never will be a cure-all for the boring speaker. But by assuming the proper mental set, you can do much to get the most from even the most tedious talker.

"I used to attend lots of outside lectures—most of them pretty uninteresting," an ex-teacher says. "Then I found that I was able to get something out of even the dullest lecture by getting myself in the right frame of mind."

Before a meeting, she would find out everything she could about the speaker—his education, work, interests, and so forth. If possible, she'd bone up on the subject, too. "By being reasonably familiar with the subject and the speaker," she says, "I am able to think ahead, draw conclusions, even second-guess the speaker. This makes the talk more interesting. And it's easy to pay attention to—and remember—something you're interested in."

The average speaker gives you abundant opportunity to go through these mental gymnastics. He talks at a rate of 120 to 180 words a minute, authorities say, while the average listener can understand the message at rates of up to 800 words a minute, and in some cases possibly more.

This means that during most talks, you'll have plenty of time to idle your mental motor. It is usually during these lulls that your fancy roams.

Another tip: look directly at the speaker when he's speaking. Close visual attention contributes to concentrated listening. It is quite difficult to look at another object and actually hear what the speaker has to say.

Learning to listen attentively is still another *must* in developing an instant memory. The super-salesman is not necessarily the best talker, but almost invariably, the best listener—thus, he is likely to remember more.

4. *Reading rapidly*. A successful lawyer told me he often had a difficult time paying attention while reading "nonlegal material." "How rapidly do you read?" I asked. He replied that in his business he had to read everything slowly and "really concentrate."

We generally agreed that most of his legal reading could be classified as difficult, requiring a relatively slow reading rate. But the lawyer did concede the possibility that other types of reading could be done at a faster pace.

He enrolled in an executive speed-reading course. A few months later, he found himself racing through newspaper and magazine columns at 700 to 800 words a minute—and often faster—with little if any loss in comprehension. "Reading at this rate," he said, "you hardly have time to do anything other than concentrate on the subject at hand."

Surprisingly, reading experts have found that needlessly slow reading is perhaps the chief cause for wool-gathering while reading. And daydreaming is the nemesis of concentration.

The proper mental set is also important to concentration while reading. This involves reading with a purpose, resting at intervals, and reading selectively.

Thus another milestone you must pass on your way to an instant memory is the ability to read rapidly, when appropriate, and well.

5. *Scheduling your time*. A personnel manager of a large depart-

ment store claims he gets "perpetual energy" by judiciously scheduling his work.

"I always try to keep three or four projects going at the same time," he says. "When I get tired of one, I go to another. I also try to alternate a hard job with an easy one, or a pleasant one with a less desirable one. Much of the fatigue we feel in everyday work is actually boredom. And one of the best ways to fight boredom is to change activities."

His scheduling further entails setting up his most difficult or least-liked chores for his high-energy periods in the day. Conversely, he slates the easy tasks (usually those he is more interested in) for the low-energy periods.

And regardless of the daily schedule, this busy executive finds that occasional breaks can often revive interest and stimulate greater concentration. The 10-minute coffee break is a well-conceived idea. One psychologist proved that most recovery from fatigue resulting from mental work happened in the first 10 minutes of rest.

6. *Working rapidly.* A sales executive who travels a great deal admitted that he literally hated to tackle the backlog of paper work which stacked up while he was away on business trips.

The paper work was not large by any standard, but it was indeed an awesome sight to him. He would spend hours wading through the task—fuming, fretting, and procrastinating—everything that a person who isn't interested does when staving off an unpleasant chore.

Now he does the same work in half the time, and with infinitely less fuss. How? "By diving into it and working like the devil," he boasts. "The faster I work, the more efficiently I seem to be able to do the paper work. In fact, I work so fast that I scarcely have time to think of how unpleasant the job really is."

He never reached the point of "liking" the periodic paper work. But his confidence in his ability to wade through it rapidly was greatly enhanced. The advantage is obvious—save time, save money.

7. *Breaking the job down.* The 90-pound weakling is habitual-

ly depicted as wanting to "whittle the big beach bully down to his size." Unfortunately, the size of the bully often makes the idea impractical.

Many of us have this same feeling when we are confronted with a formidable business chore. But, in many cases, we *can* whittle the chore down. The idea is to break the job down into smaller, more meaningful parts.

A professor-author I know practices this idea when tackling a tome of some length. "By writing the book a chapter at a time," he says, "I find it much easier to concentrate on one aspect of the overall subject. Then, in the end, I have only the mopping-up operation; you know, tying the loose ends together."

The same idea can often be applied to many workaday chores. You can concentrate more effectively on part of a task because it's simpler.

8. *Taking action.* We don't often consider the "thinking man" a man of action. Rodin's *The Thinker* is supposed to be the true picture of a man deep in thought—solemn, brow wrinkled, chin thoughtfully resting on the hand.

Nonsense, say modern psychologists. The person who is really paying attention is more often than not doing it effortlessly. His thoughts flow freely and easily. The wrinkled brow and pained expression usually signal the warm-up period, which comes before true concentration.

"My secretary told me that I pace the floor like a wounded lion when dictating," one executive says. "So I tried to dictate from my swivel chair. The results were nearly disastrous. In the sitting position, my mind went blank. But once I got back into action, the ideas seemed to flow freely."

You do not have to look far, either, to find a speaker who depends on gestures to get his ideas across. These actions actually help him to think. "Tie his hands and he'd be speechless," is the customary gibe thrown his way.

Still others swing a leg, tap a pencil, or drum fingers on a table—all for the sake of pure concentration. However, this may not be the best way to win friends and influence your boss.

9. *Exercising your mind.* Can you improve your ability to concentrate by "practicing"? Many say you can.

"I practice concentration by trying to pay strict attention to a different subject every day," one sales executive says. "I think about the subject from every possible angle, seeing it in as many lights as possible. Having done this for some months, I find that I can concentrate intensely for from 10 to 30 minutes on just about any subject I choose."

If this feat appears overly simple, try this easy one: Close your eyes and count to 100, visualizing each number as you go. You're above average if you can go the route without letting an outside thought slip in.

Walter B. Pitkin, former Columbia University journalism professor and author, used several similar "exercises" which he claimed helped improve his power to pay attention.

Among other routines, he would play a phonograph record while studying something fairly difficult. When the tune ended, he'd recite aloud to himself what he had been studying. He said this forced him to "blot out sounds to such a degree that I became virtually deaf to them."

There are many other such exercises. One of the more popular ones is to work out a not-too-easy math problem in your head.

Just for fun, why don't you try a few of these attention exercises along with your daily push-ups? And while you're at it, give serious thought to some of the concentration techniques used by others.

Perhaps there is no more single important step in developing your instant memory power than to train yourself to concentrate efficiently, even under adverse conditions.

The person with an average memory concentrates well enough, all right. But it is the person who learns to heighten this ability who develops a truly powerful instant memory.

Using Your Senses to Create Instant Memory Storage 4

Berol, an immigrant, tried many jobs after reaching America in the 1920s. He was discharged in every case, legend has it, because of his erratic memory. Skid-row bound, Berol began searching the library for a solution. Ultimately, he developed his own recall system and became known as the premier "memory expert" of New York City.

True, Berol could perform impressive memory feats, but his system was based almost entirely on mnemonics. It was so cumbersome that much of his advice would be passé today. For example, Berol warned against "writing anything down." "Trust entirely in your memory," he said. "This is the only way you can develop confidence in it."

Writing It Down

Good advice for the stone age, but not for modern times. Educators tell us to "write it down" today for at least two good reasons: first, the written word is usually a much more *reliable* reminder than an attempt at total recall; second, we generally learn better when more than one sense organ is brought into play. The so-called sensory approach to memory power involves using as many senses as possible in any learning situation.

Using All Your Senses

Seeing, hearing, touching, tasting, and smelling—these are the main avenues through which intelligence and sensations flow to the memory centers in the brain. The eyes and ears are, of course, the super-highways through which most of us acquire perhaps 95% or more of our knowledge. Touch, taste, and smell are the side roads through which sensations and impressions are perceived. In addition, many psychologists theorize that muscle or motor memory—the kinesthetic sense—is involved extensively in remembering. An outfielder, for example, must instantly compute distance, velocity, wind, and other factors in chasing a long fly ball. His muscular memory surely serves in large part as his guide.

A speaker often is able to do a better job if performing in the room where he practiced. Tests have shown that a student often does better if he takes an exam in the same room in which he studied. There is evidence that these revived "postures and movements" are effective aids to recall. The theory is that motor skills involve actions of muscles, tendons, and joints when directed toward a familiar and purposeful action.

The senses can logically be called the "tools" of memory. And it is the person who makes the effort to sharpen these sensory tools who develops instant memory power. Unfortunately, evidence abounds that the average person uses only a fraction of his sensory capabilities. As William James said, the average person uses only 10 to 15% of his overall mental ability ... including, no doubt, sensory abilities.

Helen Keller still stands as perhaps the most inspiring example of how efficiently sensory powers can be used. From infancy, she could not see, hear, or talk. Yet she was able to later graduate from Radcliffe College with high honors. She loved to hear a cat "purr" and a dog "bark." Her sense of touch was amazingly developed. She said of Mark Twain's handshake, "I feel the twinkle of his eyes." Other handshakes she found to be an impertinence.

Combining Senses

Again, an instant memory power can result from not only utilizing our eyes and ears more effectively, but using them in combination—a multiple sensory approach—when possible. Gentleman Jim Farley uses such a multiple approach in remembering names. On being introduced, Farley repeats the name several times, making a strong auditory impression (normally, I think you'll agree, we hear the name only once, and then often incorrectly). Farley is also adept at making meaningful associations with the name, a technique we'll explore later. Then, if he really wants to retain the name, he writes it down. In this manner, he can *see* the name, bringing into play the all-important visual sense. Thus Farley gets maximum mileage from his senses when applying the multiple approach to the difficult technique of name-remembering.

Farley's feats seem like "magic" to the individual who uses his memory capabilities at half-throttle. In reality, comparable feats are well within the grasp of those who will strive for instant memory power.

Dr. Wilse Webb of the U.S. Navy School of Aviation Medicine found that airmen learn much faster when they use both their eyes and ears in learning. Educators and trainers in business and industry have come to the same conclusion. Rarely today is a report, proposal, or sales presentation given which does not use effective visual aids to reinforce the spoken word. It's simply a case where "draw me a picture" pays dividends. The customer, in most such instances, understands, remembers—and frequently accepts—the presentation.

How Note-Taking Helps

Note-taking is almost always a helpful memory aid. In addition to hearing the spoken word, you use visual and perhaps muscular sensory perception in writing. Jotting down important dates, facts, and ideas as they occur would seem a *must* for the busy manager who is bombarded with hundreds of messages daily. Tests have shown conclusively that even the most efficient remember only a comparatively small segment of what they see and hear. Further, we misremember in many cases and tend to fill in our memory with ideas that coincide with our particular prejudices or mental set. Effectively taken, notes can serve as ammunition at the conference table or when writing a directive. Without notes, the executive may rely on a brilliant, but erratic memory. As Alex Osborn, the advertising genius, said: "Pencils can serve as crowbars."

"Taking notes at a conference forces me to distill and summarize as I go along," one veteran hospital administrator says. "In summarizing, I must state the gist of the message in my own words, and this usually gives them more meaning. Most important, it gives me a permanent record to refer to."

Many professional people find it equally advantageous to take notes while reading. Mortimer J. Adler, author of *How to Read a Book* (Simon and Schuster, New York, 1940), said: "I read sitting up at my desk and almost always with a pencil in hand and a pad at the side ... thinking usually tends to express itself overtly in language. One tends to verbalize ideas, questions, and difficult judgments that occur in the course of thinking. If you have been reading, you must have been thinking; you have something you can express in words.

"Some people are able to use their memory in such a way that they need not bother with notes. Again, this is a matter of individual difference. I find it more efficient not to burden my memory while reading and to use the margins of the book or a jot pad instead. The work of memory can be undertaken later, and, of course, should be. But I find it easier not to let it interfere with the work of understanding, which constitutes the main task of reading. ... You will be able to tell whether you have been reading actively by your pencil-and-paper work."

Osborn's note-taking, on the other hand, applied to his particular specialty of applied imagination. He admits that notes, taken sometimes surreptitiously in a church pew, or on a dark veranda, or even a golf course, later served as fuel for his creative imagination.

How Reciting Helps

If note-taking helps create a stronger visual impression, then talking or *reciting* reinforces impressions made through the ears. Abraham Lincoln, among others, preferred to study aloud a great deal of the time. He said it gave him the benefit of both *hearing* and *seeing* the material, thus enhancing memory. Indeed, some psychologists say that sensations or muscles used in talking are actually helpful in remembering. And many find it helpful to use "talking muscles" when trying to do hard thinking.

Numerous tests by Arthur I. Gates of Columbia University tend to prove that recitation plays an important role in remembering efficiently. Students were asked to read and reread passages as many times as possible in a certain time period. Then they progressively reduced reading time and increased recitation time. Students who read only 20% of the time and recited 80% of the time recalled nearly twice as many facts four hours later as they did when they had read the entire time.

Recitation is an art in itself and requires cultivation. First, Gates said, you must perfect the technique of recalling material in well-organized form. Then you must quickly learn to find places where material cannot be recalled. In this manner, reciting can help you readily pinpoint memory soft spots.

Some educators suggest that when studying to retain "permanently," you should pause from time to time to recite the gist of what you have read. Putting the writer's ideas into your own words forces attention and affords a realistic test of comprehension. The technique may cramp your style if you're a "super" speed-reader, but you'll almost certainly make a stronger sensory impression on your memory.

Most adults won't be able to use their sensory powers as efficiently as Helen Keller did, of course. But perhaps you can routinely use your eyes (for observation) and ears (for listening) more efficiently and thus sharpen your most important memory tools—the tools with which you can forge the foundation for your instant memory power.

Sharpening Your Listening Skill

Until recently, relatively little attention was paid to the skill of listening, as such. Most of us just assumed that we were pretty good listeners. Then educators like Dr. Ralph Nichols and Ned Flanders of the University of Minnesota came up with some significant findings. The essence of their reports is that most of us *hear,* all right, but we rarely *listen* with anything approaching maximum efficiency.

Dr. Flanders' survey told him that college professors talk about 80% of the classroom time, and that the typical college student is "hard pressed" to retain a fifth of what he hears. What is it like in business and industry? How does the typical manager spend his day? Dr. Paul Rankins of Ohio State University studied the habits of 65 managers in depth and found that the average manager spends 70% of his time—roughly 7 of every 10 minutes—communicating. Manager communication breaks down this way: 9% writing, 16% reading, 30% talking, and 45% listening. Instant memory power, needless to point out, is inextricably interwoven with all these basic skills.

How efficiently do managers listen? Not very well, if they're anything like college students. Dr. Nichols found that a group of selected freshmen, after listening to a short series of lectures, could remember only about half of what they heard immediately thereafter; a few weeks later, they could recall only a fourth of that. His conclusion: the average person operates at only about

Using Your Senses to Create Instant Memory Storage

25% of total efficiency when it comes to listening. It is significant to note that a test in listening is, in effect, a test in remembering.

"Strangely enough," one sales manager concluded, "our top salesmen aren't necessarily our best talkers. They're almost always our best listeners."

Tips for Effective Listening

Any attempt to improve your listening habits, then, automatically becomes an attempt to improve the manner in which you assimilate and retain information. Psychologists and educators pass on these tips for more efficient remembering and listening:

• *Assume the proper listening posture.* Again, the appropriate mental set should put you in the proper mood to listen. Complaints like, "My boss just won't listen," and "He only hears what he wants to hear," are heard all too frequently in business and industry. Such comments are symptoms of poor listening habits and call for immediate corrective action. The first essential ingredient in listening—and super-power remembering—is to show proper interest. This entails finding a motive, which can often be found by asking such questions as: "What is he trying to tell me?" "Why?" "How does this tie in with what I already know about the subject?" These and other queries can get you in the right frame of mind to listen attentively, and perhaps remember better.

• *Listen with an open mind.* "This guy's a dummy; he can't possibly tell me anything." You've undoubtedly "listened" to someone while in this frame of mind. What will you likely remember about the conversation? Probably only your preconceived notion that he's a dullard. Will Rogers, you'll recall, found that everyone was smarter than he was in some respect. Perhaps we should do no less. Too often we literally tune a person out, making it impossible to "hear," much less remember, what he said. Psychologists say we unwittingly pick and choose in a conversation so that we remember details in a form that agrees with our beliefs. We also tend to forget what is not in harmony with them. For example, a manager who believes he runs a "democratic organization" and pays above-average wages, may be reluctant to listen to a complaint about poor working conditions. It simply won't register with him. It is difficult, too, to recall accurately when under stress. Many emotions have an adverse effect on remembering, including anxiety, apprehension, confusion, depression, embarrassment, frustration, grief, hatred, injured pride, lack of confidence, stage-fright, and shame. Under these conditions, you're probably only half-listening, at best.

• *When possible, write it down.* This isn't always possible in the workaday world. In many cases, however, you can jot down a few notes shortly after the fact, before memory traces fade. If it's an appointment or date, almost assuredly you'll want to make a note. If it's a new word on company policy, perhaps you'll want, very briefly, to write down the gist of the matter. Your memory is capable of misremembering in whole or in part, so notes can serve as *accurate* reminders. Most business meetings beg for note-taking; so do conferences, orientation meetings, and sales presentations. Some have found it helpful to use two sheets of paper for recording a speech. On one sheet, list main ideas; on the other, "new facts." Review these sheets later and make a concerted effort to record mentally the significant facts and points. The virtue of writing it down is to force concentration, crystallize your own thinking, and reinforce memory. This effort will give you a sense of participation and effort. And, more often than not, it will lead to a thorough understanding of the salient points discussed.

• *Finally, show you're interested.* Especially in conversation, it's important to show you're a good listener. How? By assuming a posture of interest. Look interested. Nod understandingly from time to time. Agree—or disagree! Ask cogent questions. A well-timed question is proof-positive that you're listening. Forming these questions also helps you bridge the "understanding gap," the often deadly gap that separates rate of speech and rate of comprehension. As a listener, you normally assimilate information about four times faster than the average speaker can talk. What better way to use this mental time on your hands than to think about the subject and ask timely questions. It'll make you a good listener and add mileage to your memory.

Tips for Instant Memory Power Observation

The ability to observe accurately is another prerequisite for instant memory power. If you hope to observe with a high degree of accuracy, you must train yourself to be more sensitive to the world about you. Psychologists offer these suggestions for observation:

• *See things objectively.* As in listening, we often perceive things not necessarily as they actually are, but as we would like them to be. And this is the way we normally remember them. Freud was an antique collector. "When walking through the streets of a strange city," he said, "I read *antiques* in every sign that showed the slightest resemblance to the word." He also described a woman patient who was quite anxious to have children. She had the habit of reading *stork* for *stock,* a human but inaccurate observation. Probably most of us have our share of "antiques" and "storks" stashed away in our memory. To observe objectively, we must be careful not to let prejudice and faulty notions result in faulty memory.

• *Be prepared to "see."* As in all mental activity, mental set plays an important part not only in what we remember, but in how we remember it. Rolland L. Soule, associate director of Southern Police Institute, University of Louisville, trains officers to look for quick and positive identification, a task that is singularly difficult for the average citizen. He admonishes his students to carry around in their minds "mental pictures" of the objects, items, persons, and things they want to identify. When they actually see the object, the preformed mental picture in their mind's eye strikes a familiar associative note, which enables them to identify the object or person. Thus, having a reasonably accurate mental picture of a face or object, coupled with a readiness to observe, can result in highly effective observation. This principle will be especially important in the technique used to remember names and faces.

• *Make notes, mental and real.* For years, bricklayers used an average of 18 movements in laying each brick. Then Frank B. Gilbreth, an industrial engineer, found each brick could be put in place in only five movements. He did this by taking many reels of motion pictures showing bricklayers in action. He analyzed their movements and finally evolved his time-saving technique. In most businesses, a systematic observation of work methods and procedures can almost invariably produce cheaper, more efficient ways of doing business. And the camera's memory is virtually fail-proof. Many acts have been staged to test the accuracy of observation. One such test reveals that even trained, "objective" psychologists can have their problems. At an international conclave in Germany, a clown and another man rushed into a lecture room unexpectedly and started fighting. The clown knocked the other man down, then shot him. After the "murder," both men got to their feet and scrambled from the room. How did the psychologists "see" it? Only six gave reasonably accurate accounts of what happened; 24 were about half-right in the recollection; and ten gave accounts which were highly embellished with erroneous information.

Had the audience been properly *set* for the occasion, and had they been allowed to take notes, perhaps they would have observed—and remembered—more accurately.

As you sharpen your memory tools, your senses, you are perhaps ready to investigate an extension of your sensory powers—your ability to visualize in your mind's eye.

Visualization, coupled with association of objects and ideas, can work seeming miracles in the abstract areas of memory.

Remember, your senses are the prime tools you'll use in fashioning your instant memory. Hone them to the sharpest possible point.

Making Your Mind Work Like a Computer with Instant Memory Power 5

M an's mind is like a computer; it contains a record of all the things of which he was once aware. This is the interesting theory of Dr. Penfield, director of the Montreal Neurological Institute, and he makes a convincing case.

Dr. Penfield has worked with epileptic patients for over 25 years. A typical case is that of a 14-year-old girl whom we shall call Marilyn. She complained of periodic seizures which invariably were preceded by an hallucination. In the scene, she was walking across a meadow, pursued by a man with a bag. He stopped her and told her he had snakes in the bag. She became terrified and ran toward home. As it turned out, this was a true happening, which her family corroborated in detail.

In an operation, Dr. Penfield mapped out a section of Marilyn's brain and stimulated it with a sort of electronic shock pencil. Stimulating this part of her memory evoked the entire episode. After several operations, she was cured.

"One must conclude," Dr. Penfield says, "that there is hidden away in the brain a record of the stream of consciousness. It seems to hold the detail of that stream as laid down during each man's waking, conscious hours. This is not memory as we usually use the word, although it may have a relation to it. No man can recall by voluntary effort such wealth of detail. Most things that a man is able to recall to memory are generalizations and summaries. If it were not so, we might find ourselves confused, perhaps, by too great a richness of detail."

The Psychology of Remembering

Dr. Penfield's theory offers little basis for practical memory development. But his work does afford an excellent example of two principles which apparently are constantly at work in remembering: association and visualization. Simply stated, association involves linking objects together that occur together. Visualization or imaging is simply "seeing" something in your mind's eye—a mental picture.

In Marilyn's case, visualizing the black bag triggered a stream of consciousness which included her traumatic experience from childhood. In this state, she could visualize the event in detail. What caused the image to appear in the first place can no doubt be traced to a sensory sensation—something she saw, heard, felt, smelled, or tasted. Most of us are guilty of such associative mental meanderings every day. For example, we catch a sniff of a certain type of perfume and immediately visualize the girl who used to wear that perfume. Then, through association, we recall all sorts of related events—a football game, a college prom, a certain professor, any number of things. All that is needed to unreel these vignettes from life, according to Dr. Penfield, is the proper stimulus. This can come from a myriad of things we perceive through one of the five senses, and all our senses apparently work in combination in forming "memory." It is difficult, for example, to visualize yourself standing at the seashore, without at the same time *hearing* the pounding of waves on the beach, *feeling* salt spray, and *smelling* the briny ocean.

Obviously, the thinking person routinely associates and visualizes almost continuously during his waking hours. He carries out these mental functions automatically. But it is the man who can develop and heighten his awareness of these traits who is on his way to developing an instant memory power.

Historically, the principles of association were laid down by Aristotle and Plato. They were elaborated upon by the British school of associationists, including John Locke, James Mills, and David Hartley, in the early 1800s. It wasn't until 1890, however, that William James set down his often-quoted observations in his *Principles of Psychology*.

"In mental terms," James wrote, "the more other facts a fact is associated with in the mind, the better possession of it our memory retains. Each of its associates becomes a hook to which it hangs, a means to fish it up by when sunk beneath the surface. Together they form a network of attachments by which it is woven into the entire tissue of our thought. The secret of a good memory is thus the secret of forming diverse and multiple associations with every fact we care to retain.

"But in the forming of associations with a fact, what is it but thinking about the fact as much as possible. Briefly, then of two men with the same outward experiences and the same amount of mere native tenacity, the one who thinks over his experiences most and weaves them into systematic relations with each other will be the one with the best memory."

James' theory again supports the point that the average man is using only a fraction of his instant memory power; thus, the man who disciplines his memory—trains it, if you will—is the one who will develop instant memory power.

Psychologists like Harry L. Hollingsworth carry association a step further in coining the word "redintegration." One impression, he says, evokes not a single associated idea, but the whole situation of which both formerly were a part.

Hollingsworth, in *Psychology of Thought,* says he used "redintegration" in remembering names and faces. "I think of objects and events which are not present—say a number of people I have known. How can I do this? A simple way would be for part of each person to be at hand, say each man's hat, or perhaps his physiognomy. I may use names which have been associated with the men, speaking, writing, or looking at them. Or I may take attitudes in each case, characteristic of the way in which each person has affected me; I may experience what I call feelings, appropriate to each. Or if I have visual imagery at my command, such imagery may also be employed." Thus photograph, name, gesture, attitude, feeling, and image all had meaning to him. Any of these elements could "redintegrate" or call to mind the person or event it symbolized. Any or all of these items may function in the thinking process.

Principles of Association

James thought of association as the "law of neural habit." In other words, things seen and heard together cohere with each other and are remembered in this way. Others have elaborated, too extensively in some cases, upon the subject. For practical purposes, the laws of association can be narrowed down into those of *similarity, opposites,* and *togetherness.* A simple word-association test can illustrate the point.

What is the first thing that comes to mind when you see the word *Waterloo?* Write it down. Now do the same thing for these words: *Juliet, tall, good, cigar, clouds.*

Perhaps your answers went something like this: *Waterloo* evoked the response *Napoleon,* while *Juliet* reminded you of *Romeo.* These responses would be based on the so-called law of togetherness: Things which habitually occur together in time or space are generally remembered together. The mention of one thing will bring to mind the other.

For *tall* perhaps you responded with *short;* for *good, bad.* Obviously, the principle of opposites is at work here: one subject will bring to mind another which is diametrically opposed in meaning. And finally, the principle of similarity: similar things are remembered together if they're alike in meaning. *Cigar,* for example, likely brought to mind *cigarette, tobacco,* or a similar response. Perhaps *clouds* evoked the response *rain.* There is one other aspect of this latter principle which bears mentioning. Objects may be easily remembered together if they *sound* alike: *moon-June, bat-rat.* The rhyme makes them linger in memory, just as it is easy to learn a doggerel like "candy is dandy, but liquor is quicker."

These principles—similarity, opposites, togetherness—can in no way literally be called laws, because they are not invariable. One word will not always evoke the same response. Your reaction depends on a number of factors, like mood, locale, and time of day. But responses can, in many cases, be made reasonably predictable if conscious effort is put forth to create an association based on one of these principles. This will be demonstrated later when remembering names and faces and other abstract facts.

On a practical basis, you can use association successfully to remember many of the facts and ideas it is necessary for you to use in your daily routine. When you need to retain a bit of information, automatically relate the incoming message to your existing knowledge of the subject. As Dr. Penfield says, "When we make a decision or are called on to relate an experience, there is a key somewhere in the temporal lobes of the brain which swiftly scans the past, allowing us better to judge the present."

How Your Subconscious Uses Association

Very likely, your subconscious uses association routinely in helping you make decisions and carry out daily assignments. A personnel manager, for example, cannot make a decision on his company's hiring policy without comparing it—associating it—with all factors known about the company policy. In addition, he will mentally review what he knows about other companies' policies. Only when he explores these factors can he come up with a well-thought-out decision. Undoubtedly, he can associate even more effectively by creating a high degree of awareness of the power of association of ideas. He can often ask questions which will literally force him to associate. Has this policy been used before? Where? By whom? To what degree did it succeed or fail? What are the implications locally? Perhaps all these questions can't be answered, indicating research might be necessary before a judicious decision could be reached.

Decisions requiring a creative twist can benefit even more by association of ideas. The technique is aptly demonstrated by Osborn, the advertising innovator. One of his many novel ideas was to make manikins out of rubber so they could be shipped flat and later be inflated and used in a window. Plaster manikins were more expensive and costly to ship, and easier to break. How did he conceive this idea? By a little free-wheeling association.

While in the dentist's chair, his hand touched the little rubber tube connecting the chair to a Bunsen burner. Touching the rubber reminded him of the big balloons in the shape of full-size ships, tanks, and guns which had been used to fool the Nazis on the eve of the Normandy invasion. "These ideas flashed across my mind in less than a second," he admitted. From the balloons, his mind turned quickly from the models of weapons to the models in a window display he had visited a few days before. "Even as my mind worked in that roundabout way, I analyzed my mental gyrations and within the same hour started to write them down. Production of ideas depends on the content of your mind and how you mix these ingredients. Association of ideas serves as a catalyst in this process." (*Applied Imagination,* Charles Scribner's Sons, 1953.)

The principle can be used not only in an advertising agency, but also in a business or industry requiring a new slant, a new way to get sales, or a new product to sell. The formula is simple. Give your top executives a problem. Then put them in a room and ask them to express any ideas they have on the subject, even if the ideas seem to be ridiculous. The technique is called "brainstorming," and many companies have found it effective. The game is based entirely on association of ideas. One person will make a suggestion, which in turn evokes an associated response from another, and still another. The relevancy of the ideas is not considered at the moment. Later, the ideas are analyzed and many are discarded. But quite often, such sessions will result in *the* idea which proves to be a time-saver or a money-maker. Sharpening your ability to associate meaningfully and imaginatively are big steps toward acquiring that instant memory power.

The Process of Visualization

The process of visualization is relatively easy to describe. When you get up at night in the dark and bump into an object, you probably "recognize" it by picturing it in your mind's eye. You probably find it difficult to hear the distant sound of a train whistle without visualizing a train speeding down the railroad line. Probably most people see many hundreds, possibly thousands of "pictures" during any given hour. The value of this phenomenon, however, is difficult to assess, since mental pictures can't be viewed objectively. Also, some people are more adept at visualizing than others.

In fact, psychologists have long debated the part visualization may or may not play in the thinking process. Alfred Binet, originator of the intelligence test, concluded that images or mental pictures were not essential to thinking. Others, like Woodworth and Edward B. Titchener, came to the same conclusion.

On the other hand, Sir Frederick Bartlett, professor of psychology at Cambridge, looked extensively into imaging or visualization and came to some interesting conclusions. "Visual pictures," he wrote, "may have a very wide range of serviceableness when the task is to describe, or to recall individual objects or events. Words or phrases may very likely have a less wide descriptive range, but may be superior when it comes to the question of establishing an accurate order or sequence." (*Remembering,* Cambridge University Press, 1967.)

Bartlett and others claim that some people can be classified as visualizers (they remember best by seeing), while vocalizers remember best by hearing. Probably, most learn by using a combination of these two senses—a multiple sensory approach.

How Visualization Helps

Visualizers, Bartlett found, have greater confidence in their ability to remember, say, a list of items. Seeing the picture in their mind's eye gives them confidence that they are correct in their answer. To them, "seeing is believing." Vocalizers lack this confidence, but apparently do a better job of remembering things in order.

He also found that things that have comical significance are retained so long as the comical meaning is remembered. Proper names, for example, which tend to produce laughter, are more likely to be remembered. But they are also more likely to be transformed in the recollection.

There is evidence that visualization does play a considerable part in some aspects of memory. Artur Rubinstein's feats of memory are legendary and may be a case in point. In 1903 he caused a sensation in Warsaw by performing Paderewski's *Sonata in E Flat Minor* the day after it was published. He learned Cesar Franck's complex *Symphonic Variations* on the train en route to a concert hall in Madrid. And he can commit a sonata to memory in one hour.

When Rubinstein plays, he turns the pages in his mind. He is said to remember the smallest detail, like a coffee stain at the bottom of a page, or a note scribbled in the margin. At breakfast he might start a Brahms symphony in his head. If he is called to the phone and hangs up an hour later, he discovers the symphony has been going on all the time and he is in the final movement.

Rubenstein's "music images" may be a singular talent. But psychologist G.H. Betts claims that subjects who have clearest imagery for one sense have good imagery for voices, music, odors, tastes, and other sensory associations.

Photographic Memory

Visualization carried to the extreme degree is called photographic memory, or eidetic imagery. The consensus of psychologists is that few, if any, can literally photograph in their mind's eye the exact content of entire printed pages. Tests have shown that if there is such a thing as photographic memory, it is more likely to exist in children. In one experiment, Gordon W. Allport had 30 English children look at a picture of a German street scene for half a minute. There was a word in the scene, *Gartenwirthschaft*, which appeared over a building. Later, in recalling what they had seen in the picture, some could read off the German word, even though they did not understand the language. A few could even spell it backward.

Visual pictures, in many cases, are the stuff of which dreams are made. Joseph Hastrow has found that dreams depend mostly on sensory experiences. Testing blind persons, he found that no person blinded before the age of five had visual pictures in his dreams; those who became blind after age seven all had visual images in their dreams.

In the realm of ideas, we can only conjecture as to the role played by our ability to visualize. Some psychologists contend the ability to "see" an abstract idea makes it more understandable. One form of visualization, structural visualization, is characteristic of successful engineers, physicists, scientists, aviators, and others, points out Johnson O'Connor, founder of the Human Engineering Laboratory. "This ability," he says, "is an inherent sense for three-dimensional forms . . . an instinctive ability to construct in the mind's eye from a flat blueprint, a clear picture of a solid object."

The ability to visualize accurately might also explain the feats of many "mentalists" like George Bidder. Asked to multiply in his head, say, 89 times 73, he would immediately give the correct answer: 6,497. He did this mentally by multiplying 80 times 70, 80 by 3, 9 by 70, and 9 by 3. He visualized the products—5,600, 240, 630, and 27—in his head and came up with the answer. This ability is usually linked to a person of high intelligence, but not necessarily. Psychologists tell us of "idiot savants," persons with relatively low IQs who are able to perform mental feats which are usually mechanical and mathematical in nature.

Combining Visualizing and Associating

If visualization's precise role in higher thinking is sometimes difficult to pinpoint, it is simple to demonstrate how visual pictures can be utilized in remembering specific events, particularly when used with an effective association.

The essence of association, you'll recall, is to link the newly acquired fact or object with something already known. In so doing, you must, of course, picture the objects involved in your mind's eye. It is further helpful to make these mental pictures as vivid as possible, since "unusual" things are more easily remembered than the commonplace. You'll remember something that is moving more easily than a static object. And remember Bartlett's suggestion: make it funny.

An Experiment You Can Perform

To illustrate the principles of association and visualization as related to remembering a series of disconnected objects, try the following experiment.

Step one is to substitute ten objects, which can be readily visualized, for numbers, which are abstract and hard to remember. For the number 1, substitute the word *hat*. Make this a specific mental picture and place the hat in a fixed place. This makes the object better "known" and easier to associate with. Try to visualize these specific mental pictures for the other nine numbers: 2, *hen;* 3, *ham;* 4, *hair;* 5, *hill;* 6, *hedge;* 7, *hook;* 8, *hive;* 9, *hoop;* 10, *toes.* The reason for selecting these specific objects will be explained in the following discussion of mnemonic techniques. For the time being, simply accept the objects at face value. Now, review the list and make the item as specific as you possibly can. Once you have firm mental pictures in mind for each of the above items, you're ready to associate a list of virtually anything. For simplicity's sake, let's take a list of ten tasks for tomorrow.

1. Have the *typewriter* repaired. When the number "1" is mentioned, immediately revert to your familiar mental picture of

Making Your Mind Work Like a Computer with Instant Memory Power 57

the *hat*. Now add the new element, a typewriter. Keeping the *hat* in place, literally force the typewriter atop it and have someone typing away with tremendous speed (action). It's a rather unusual sight, and this fact should make it easy to remember.

2. Draft a *speech* for the Lion's Club. A speech is the main idea here, and you'll want to tie it into your second word picture, a *hen*. In this case have your *hen* flailing away in her best southern oratory, speaking no less to a group of real lions.

3. Update *production charts*. First, visualize your picture substitute for number 3, *ham*. Now inject the new element, a visual picture of a chart. Stick it with pins or throw darts at it to symbolize the idea of updating the charts.

4. *Lunch* with the president. *Hair* is the picture substitute, and it's quite simple to visualize you and your boss dining there. (Be careful, of course, not to get in your boss' hair.) Your mental image, fortunately, is your own. No one need ever know how you remembered it.

5. Call your *stockbroker*. At the command, number 5, visualize your familiar *hill*. Now inject the something new, in this case a ticker-tape symbolic of the stock market. Have it moving at a fast rate, literally covering the hillside with ticker tape. A vivid and memorable mental picture.

6. Clean out *personal files*. *Hedge* is the word to be used in the association. Insert an oversized version of your personal filing cabinet, and picture yourself removing the content frantically, strewing the place with paper until a bushy hedge is formed.

7. Interview for a new *secretary*. Whatever your *hook*, you're going to have to get it hung some place—perhaps in the secretary's dress while she's taking dictation. An interesting sight; an easy item to remember.

8. *Running* exercise. You'll have to visualize yourself in track shorts for this one. Only instead of picturing yourself at the athletic club, think of yourself orbiting the bee*hive*. With the occupants after you, you'll move out quite rapidly.

9. Have *car* repaired. Associating with a *hoop*, visualize your car running over a child's hoop, breaking down, obviously in need of repair.

10. Purchase *airline tickets*. *Toes* and airliners—how do you get them together? As a starter, try using your toes to catapult the airplane into the wild blue yonder. Or perhaps even more vivid, have the airliner crashing into your toes.

That's the assignment. Now, without referring to the list, try to remember the ten assigned items. Think of the ten basic visual substitutes for the numbers 1 through 10, and in each case try to remember the item you associated with it.

Let this exercise suffice as your first step toward developing your mnemonic or artificial memory. You will find in later chapters that once you've mastered mnemonic techniques, you will be on your way to mastering the difficult areas of memory, such as disconnected facts or ideas, numbers, names, and faces.

This will be a big step in your quest for an instant memory power.

6
Increasing Mental Efficiency with Instant Memory Power

Harold E. Burtt of Ohio State University read Greek passages to his two-year-old son daily for a period of three months. About six years later, the professor read his youngster the same Greek passages, along with some new ones. It took the eight and one-half-year-old from one-fourth to one-third fewer trials to learn the passages he had heard as an infant. Such occurrences appear to be dramatic proof that "memory traces" lurk just below the surface of consciousness.

Hermann Ebbinghaus, a German scientist, was the first to prove scientifically the "savings theory" in relearning material. He also gave credence to many common-sense observations about memory: we forget quite rapidly; something that is barely learned is generally barely remembered; it's much easier to remember material which has meaning than something that has little or no significance; and it's usually best to space learning over a period of time rather than to learn during a relatively brief period, if you want to retain the material for a long period of time.

Ebbinghaus' experiments were unique and bear brief mention. He created about 2,300 so-called nonsense syllables, such as *sef, zor, miz, juk*—"words" that had no meaning to him. He then spent over two years testing himself in learning and relearning various series of these nonsense syllables. Since the syllables had no meaning—and he created no mnemonic devices to help him remember them—he could establish a "pure" rate of forgetting on homogeneous material. He memorized at a constant rate of 150 strokes a minute as measured by a metronome at his side. And he tried to make conditions as constant as possible, skipping experiments when he was not up to par mentally or physically. Ebbinghaus' findings were published in a monograph in 1885, and he has since been regarded in psychological circles as the preeminent authority on learning and remembering.

How We Forget

Ebbinghaus' forgetting curve has served as a graphic reminder of the fallibility of human memory. On nonsense syllables, he found that you forget 41.8% of the material roughly 20 minutes after learning takes place. After an hour, the forgetting rate drops to 55.8%, and after 8.8 hours, to 64.2%. Forgetting then tapers off to 66.3% in 24 hours; 72.2% in 48 hours; 74.6% in six days; and 78.9% in a month.

In similar tests on more meaningful material, the rate of retention naturally tends to increase. But the path of the forgetting curve remains the same. Forgetting occurs rather dramatically during the first two days, or more specifically, during the first few minutes after learning, then tapers off gradually beyond that point. The message is abundantly clear—effective repetition is another key to an instant memory power. If you want to remember a speech, a name, or a fact, you must review the material as quickly as possible after initial learning takes place. And subsequent review doesn't hurt a bit.

Forgetting occurs so rapidly that you almost always have to repeat that name or fact several times. Otherwise, the information has a better-than-even chance of being relegated to the point of no return in your memory. There are exceptions, of course. You may retain information—usually interesting or vivid impressions—after a single exposure. But generally, early and periodic reviewing is an absolute necessity.

This being the case, and since you can't hope to retain everything, it follows that you should be selective in what you attempt to recall. In other words, it pays to develop a good *forgettery*. If the item does not somehow fit your needs, then by all means abandon it. And one of the best ways to forget is *not* to dwell on the matter. Simply do not repeat it.

Overlearning for Memorizing

If you do want to retain information, however, here's good news. It's normally much easier to remember the second time around. In one experiment, Ebbinghaus first learned a series of 16 syllables, considering the list of syllables "learned" when he could first repeat the list without making an error. He then tried to relearn the same series 24 hours later, and found he could do so in two-thirds of the time required the first time around—a savings in time of about one-third in relearning. Significantly, if the series was not learned in exactly the same order, there was no savings in time. The syllables, in other words, were associated in order. "Each member apparently has a tendency ... to draw after itself all the members of the series which followed it," Ebbinghaus wrote. "These tendencies are strongest for members which immediately follow."

Ebbinghaus' findings, along with subsequent discoveries by educators and experimental psychologists about learning and remembering, have given us some broad principles to use in most learning situations. These principles will help form the very basis of your instant memory power. Here they are:

• *For "permanency" you must overlearn.* If you really want to remember the content of that new company directive or the names of the new men in the territory, you'll have to work at it. Almost all information remembered indefinitely is acquired through overlearning. Consensus is that you'll have to spend, on the average, about 50% more time in repeating or using the information beyond the first correct repetition. Ebbinghaus first proved it scientifically with his nonsense syllables; anything that is barely learned is soon forgotten. There are exceptions, of course. As mentioned previously, something intensely interesting or vivid will often hang in your memory. In most cases, however, the fact must literally be drilled into the memory.

Ebbinghaus demonstrated the point by memorizing a variety of nonsense syllables, all the lists being similar in makeup. He went over one list eight times, another 16 times, and other lists in various increments up to 64 times, where he found the law of diminishing returns set in (besides, he understandably got a headache at this juncture). Ebbinghaus discovered that the percentage of time saved on each list corresponded almost exactly with the number of repetitions used on each list. When he read the list eight times, he had an 8% savings; 24 times, 23% savings; 64 times, 64% savings.

The rule of thumb is: repeat it often, remember it longer.

How to Memorize Speeches and Reports

• *Spaced learning is better than massed learning or cramming.* To remember a speech or report of any length, you must go over the paper a number of times. At what interval and at what specific time during the day is review likely to be most effective? Is it best to do most of your memory work within a relatively short period of time, or spread the job out over a longer period? The unanimous decision goes to the longer period, when practical. Experiments testing the comparative efficiency of the two methods show that spaced learning is from 12 to 15% more efficient.

Dr. Sarah McAustin, for example, hand-picked two comparable groups of students. She had one group read a technical paper five times in one day; the other group read the same paper once a day over a five-day period. The latter group's retention, as tested a month later, was 30% better than the other group's. Where a motor skill is involved, such as in learning to type, distributed practice is *far* superior, according to psychologist William F. Book.

"You can remember something better if your efforts are extended over a period of time," says an educational administrator. "Spacing provides additional time in which new ideas can 'sink in.' During this added time, you can make a more meaningful association with the new material, and there appears a strong likelihood that your subconscious mind may do some of your memory work for you."

The subconscious mind comes into play in the phenomenon called reminiscence—a spontaneous refreshing of memory.

How Reminiscence Works

A name, fact, or idea which eludes your memory sometimes comes to you "from out of the blue." Dr. Philip B. Ballard discovered this condition while having a group of London school children memorize poems. Several students remembered 25 lines shortly after initial readings. The next day, however, some of them were able to recall 26 lines, with no practice time in between to account for the improved performance. Later tests have shown that reminiscence occurs either only to a small degree or not at all in most adults, but to a greater extent in children. Seemingly, the only logical explanation for this phenomenon is that your subconscious mind works for you during periods of apparent inactivity.

Cramming, of course, can be used effectively to memorize on a crash basis. The method is particularly effective if you wish to use the information only once, as in the case perhaps of giving a special report that won't be repeated. But a great deal of information gained through cramming is forgotten shortly thereafter, as most students will attest. Spaced learning is a virtual must for remembering "for keeps."

The Best Time to Memorize

What time of day is best for carrying out a "memory assignment?" The harried working man obviously can't always control this factor. But assuming he has a choice, and if the difficulty level of the material warrants special attention, the best bet appears to be at night, just before retiring.

New impressions tend to crowd "old" ideas out—even those acquired only a few hours before. Psychologists call this *retroactive inhibition;* new facts and impressions simply inhibit or lessen chances of recalling earlier ones. For this reason, forgetting usually occurs at a slower rate in sleep than during waking hours. When awake, we are incessantly bombarded with countless impressions.

John G. Jenkins and Karl M. Dallenbach were among the first to study the effects of sleep and waking activity on newly acquired information. They concluded that most forgetting is caused by interference from new experiences rather than from the passing of time itself. German investigators found subjects recalled 56% of learned material after an interval of idleness, but only 26% when the intervening time was used for additional mental work.

Rules for Effective Studying

Considerable interference also seems to be created when assignments are similar in nature. John A. McGeoch said students find this true when studying, say, Spanish right after studying French. But studying a different type of subject, like physics or math, did not cause appreciable interference. Where possible, then, a daily schedule which alternates varied assignments tends to enhance concentration and memory.

• *Whole learning is usually better than part learning.* In remembering a piece of some length, say a poem or speech, is it best to go over it from beginning to end at each repetition? Or should you learn it a section at a time, mastering one section before moving on to the next? It depends, of course, on a number of things: complexity of material, time available, and your personal preference.

Experiments have shown that all things being equal, the whole method is more efficient, despite the fact that the part method seems to be more popular. Consensus is that in most cases, savings of 12 to 15% accrued from using the whole method.

Miss Loftie Steffens, a veteran speech counselor, says: "When a poem is learned stanza by stanza, each preceding stanza is repeated every time a recitation is made. Thus, a person will generally end up knowing the first part of the poem better than the latter parts, simply because he has repeated the earlier parts more often. Since a chain is only as strong as its weakest link, the not-so-well-learned stanzas often prove to be a real stumbling block."

The whole method theoretically leads to spending equal time on all parts of the piece, tending to establish more uniformity and coherence in learning. In any case, it's wise to skim, or preread a piece in its entirety at the outset to get a "feel" for the best route to take.

There are cases, of course, in which part learning is more desirable, particularly if certain segments of the piece have to be stressed or the piece is unusually long.

• *Practice makes perfect—or does it?* Whose picture is on a $5 bill? What color are your secretary's eyes? How many red stripes does the American flag have? Are doors leading into public buildings pushed or pulled from the outside? Which letters of the alphabet are not included on your telephone dial? If repetition alone were the answer, you would be able to answer these questions with ease. You "see" these things almost every day. But if you're like most people, you'll be hard-pressed to answer half of these questions correctly. Repetition, by itself, is clearly not a sure-fire way to a more efficient memory.

Two conditions must usually accompany the repetition for greater memory efficiency. First, the information must have real meaning; otherwise, you will only be repeating, parrot-like, a succession of words. Remembering meaningless material can obviously be done through repetition, but the effects are rarely lasting. This is why repetition alone will not always work in remembering highly abstract names and numbers. The basic problem in such cases is to somehow render such items more meaningful. Second, the information needs to be repeated with a relatively high degree of alacrity. The higher your reactivity rate (degree of mental alertness), the better your chances of grasping and retaining.

Using Self-Rewards

In addition, learning or remembering should be made as pleasant an experience as possible. Thorndike demonstrated in his work with animals, and later humans, that learning depends in large degree on the law of effect: a connection or association is made either weak or strong by the consequences of the act. If the learning process is pleasant, the connection is strengthened. An annoying state of affairs tends to decrease the ability to learn and remember. In other words, we tend to "stamp in" or "stamp out" an act from memory, according to whether the result is favorable or unfavorable.

Thorndike and others also stressed the importance of reward in furthering the learning process. A cup of coffee, a cigarette, a brief walk, an informal conversation—all of these can be rewards for a job well done. Such respites can help recharge your "mental battery."

A recharged mental battery appears to go hand-in-glove with efficient memory. Ebbinghaus, an early riser, found his memory was about 12% more efficient at 7 a.m. than at 10 p.m. "Night people" probably find the reverse true. They have a hard time remembering whether they put sugar in their coffee at breakfast.

Dr. Hans Berger, who spent over 30 years studying the nature of electrical brain waves, concluded that memory functions best under stimulation, when brain waves are emitting at a high level.

During sleep, he found, brain-wave activity is lowest—only two or three waves a second. As one awakens, the rate increases, peaking out when the individual is confronted with a difficult mental problem. When you're challenged and your brain is cooking on all four burners, your memory is usually at its very best.

Effective, meaningful repetition is another major building block in developing your instant memory.

7
Using Instant Memory Power Techniques to Read Better and Retain More

Coleridge, the British poet, said some people are "hourglass readers"—facts and ideas run out of their minds like sand and leave not a vestige behind. Conversely, he said, efficient readers are like the slaves of Golanda, who cast all worthless sand aside and retain only pure gems. "Gems," to the beleaguered businessman, are facts and ideas needed to increase overall efficiency.

Reading to retain such gems should thus become one's primary goal. The efficient reader is able to retain a good deal of what he considers meaningful. The "hourglass reader" has a memory like a sieve. But by using more effective reading techniques, he too can become a collector of gems.

Increasing Your Reading Ability

Effective reading techniques go hand-in-glove with instant memory power, since very likely a substantial part of what you want to remember must be gleaned from the printed page. Here are some reading techniques designed to increase your ability to read well and remember.

First, learn to *read with a purpose*. Sir Francis Bacon said: "Some books are to be tasted, others to be swallowed, and some few to be chewed and digested." In your daily routine, you're probably confronted with reams of reading material. Some of the material can be skimmed hurriedly and dismissed; some of it can be read for specific information—a fact here and a fact there; and some of it must be studied so that understanding of the subject is deepened.

How do you determine your purpose for reading? Usually by making a rapid, analytical appraisal of the material. Existing knowledge on the subject, of course, gives you a "lead." A quick preview of the article, paying special attention to titles, subheads, photos, and other significant markings, gives you further insight. You then skim the article at a very rapid rate, reading for main ideas and a few key facts. You probe much as a reporter does in writing an article. What is the main purpose in writing the piece? At whom is it aimed? When—how—was the information obtained? And above all, why is the article important to remember? Such queries obviously must be "personal" in nature, for you will read and remember what is important to *your* needs. Remembering, like comprehension, is almost always selective and partial.

Having thus arrived at your purpose for reading, you are now ready to select a reading "gear," a rate of speed which will enable you to remember and comprehend at the desired level of efficiency. Reading the daily newspaper provides an example of the spectrum of reading gears or skills you'll need.

Reading at an Appropriate Speed

You no doubt read many of the stories for a specific, limited purpose. For example: daily stock-market quotations, football scores, an account of a local murder trial, and random news and feature articles. You probably read these and certain other stories rather hurriedly for the most part, with little thought of retaining the information beyond tomorrow. In the same issue, however, you might elect to read quite carefully a comprehensive article about tax reforms. Assuming the article affects your job and your pocketbook, you will no doubt read with a high degree of interest. You will likely read the article at a slower rate of speed, and you will likely reread various sections several times. Many other items in the same newspaper will be read with an interest level falling somewhere in between these two extremes.

Thus, as an efficient reader, you first recognize the relative importance of the material, then read with a speed and style appropriate to your needs. These factors will generally determine to a large extent the level of comprehension and duration of retention.

How Skimming Can Improve Reading

Another technique that will help you read faster, and in some cases remember more, is that of skimming. To skim is to move your eyes across the page at a very rapid rate, reading mainly for the salient facts and ideas. The technique is especially suited to relatively easy-to-read material and to subjects that you already know a great deal about. Efficient readers can often skim at up to several thousand words a minute on familiar or "easy" material.

The main virtue of skimming is that it gives you a bird's-eye view of the subject. By reading in phrases rather than word-for-word, and by eliminating most regression (going back over the information), you can cover considerable material in a relatively short period. Perhaps you can breeze along at rates of from 1,000 to 2,500 words a minute, or even faster in exceptional cases.

But it does not stand to reason that your retention and comprehension will *increase* while reading at very rapid rates. Unfortunately, some of the super-fast "reading rates" touted commercially are in reality skimming rates. Owen Webster, the well-known British reading instructor, says that to describe reading in terms of skimming speed is meaningless. "It would," he said, "be like saying in terms of words per minute that if you take half a minute to look up a number in the Central London telephone directory, you have skimmed the directory at 17 million words a minute." (*Read Well and Remember,* Simon & Schuster, 1965.)

In perspective, skimming is a valuable tool for reviewing material and in looking for specific information or facts.

When to Read Slowly

The opposite side of the coin to skimming is reading deliberately for better retention and comprehension. If reading for thorough comprehension is your purpose, you must employ all of the techniques required for effective remembering. And remembering, you will recall, depends generally on the strength of the impression made, the nature of the association made, and the frequency with which it is made. This is the stuff which Bacon said must be "chewed and digested."

To comprehend, literally, is to grasp the meaning of, to understand. Further, there is a marked distinction between remembering and comprehending. It is possible, for example, to remember the writer's words and repeat them without understanding them. Understanding or comprehending words means not only that you can repeat them but also grasp the main ideas. You can explain what you have read in your own words, and you can apply it to other situations. Anyone who has taught, for example, has been challenged by the task of explaining an abstract thought to another. He knows it is impossible to do this effectively without fully grasping the idea and all of its ramifications. Reading to comprehend, bearing in mind that comprehension is always partial, normally requires reading at a more deliberate speed than skimming and involves different techniques.

"None of the comprehension skills will develop without conscious effort," says Dr. James E. Devine, head of the Reading Institute of New York University. "The mature reader selects, organizes, summarizes, and evaluates what he reads." The techniques involved are for fuller retention and comprehension.

One of the principal rules for effective comprehension laid down by reading experts is that you read *actively* rather than passively. Someone has suggested that, strictly speaking, all reading is active, but reading is better or worse according to whether it is more or less active. Reading actively involves all the skills

Using Instant Memory Power Techniques to Read Better and Retain More 73

required in efficient remembering—proper mental set and concentration, reading for meaning, and reviewing.

Many magazine articles, novels, and newspaper stories can be read with a relatively low reactivity rate. They pose no particular mental challenge, and often there is little to comprehend or remember. If your job, however, is virtually to digest a lengthy company directive, with an eye to complying with it, your reading reactivity rate should be something else again. In this case you must comprehend and retain ideas, along with related facts, so that you will be able to use them later on. This type of reading obviously requires a much higher level of mental activity.

Specifically, efficient readers use at least two distinct techniques to help them read actively. They systematically make notes of significant ideas and facts, and they articulate significant points occasionally while reading.

"I find it more efficient not to burden my memory while reading and to use the margins of the book or a jot pad instead," Mortimer J. Adler has said. "One of the reasons I find reading a slow process is that I keep a record of what little thinking I do. I cannot go on reading the next page if I do not make a memo of something which occurred to me in reading this one." (*How to Read a Book,* Mortimer J. Adler, 1940, Simon & Schuster.)

Writing down the main ideas of a passage, along with relevant details supporting these main ideas, should be done in a manner and style befitting the reader. Some readers like to skim an article once or twice, jotting down first the main idea, then substantiating facts. Others prefer to, in effect, outline as they go along. Whatever your style, the process of writing it down literally forces you to isolate and concentrate on the main ideas. The net result is a strong *effort* to remember. Nila Banton Smith, Director of the Reading Institute at New York City University, has a unique way of "visually" reading for ideas. "As you read," she says, "think of the main idea as a magnet drawing like particles toward it—the particles being the small detailed ideas. When you become adept at grasping clusters of details in their right relationship, you will have become a skillful reader." (*Read Faster and Get More from Your Reading,* 1958, Prentice-Hall Inc.) She suggests that the skilled reader, after a period of time, will be able to diagram these main ideas and their subplots mentally. It is perhaps significant to note again, however, that strictly from a memory standpoint, writing something down on paper theoretically has the added advantage of involving muscular or motor memory.

Reciting What You Have Read

Gates, as mentioned earlier, has said that reciting makes a strong auditory impression, thus bettering your chances to remember. This is especially true, he claims, if you want to recall material verbatim or in substance.

Psychological experiments have shown that in trying to recall a past event, there is a strong tendency to recall the dominant impression, then mentally "fill in" the blanks. An individual can quite easily delude himself into believing he remembers specific details, when, as a matter of fact, he does not. The "filling in" process is more difficult during recitation. Talking the matter out forces a moment of truth for your memory. Further, recitation has the advantage of making a strong auditory impression—an impression which apparently does not register at all or only marginally when repeating silently.

Gates' experiments with school children, you will recall, demonstrated the effects of recitation on memory. He started by having the group read silently during the entire study period. Then he progressively worked up to the point where he had them reading 20% of the time and reciting 80% of the time. Four hours later, they recalled nearly twice as many facts as a result of the latter experiments.

Recitation has the virtue of forcing you to recall information in an organized form. It also helps you develop the technique of being able to spot information quickly.

The Goal of Comprehension

Comprehension, of course, is the real goal of meaningful

reading. This is not to say that one cannot read rapidly and quite well. Most efficient readers can. But the matter of speed has perhaps been overemphasized in many cases.

In any reading course worth its salt, the principles of efficient reading for retaining and comprehension are stressed to the exclusion of speed for speed's sake. Most reputable courses take this approach: learn the principles of effective analytical reading, then speed will take care of itself. One should take such a course to develop these techniques properly.

The question of whether you can read faster and comprehend more really becomes one of semantics to a large degree. Certainly the very slow reader can often increase comprehension by speeding up his rate, since a very slow rate can thwart effective concentration. But the validity of the claim, so far as a competent reader is concerned, must finally rest upon the definition of *reading* and *comprehension.*

Leading authorities, such as Dr. George D. Spache, director of the Reading Laboratory and Clinic at the University of Florida, offer interesting insight into the matter. He defines reading as taking in more or less all words on a printed page. "Assuming that the reader can recognize and comprehend the maximum span of three words per fixation, and that there are no regressions, the line of ten words is read in .66 of a second, or at a rate of approximately 900 words per minute," Dr. Spache said. "Any speed greater than this involves omitting lines, the technique recognized by most authorities as skimming, not 'reading.' It is apparent that the upper speeds suggested as feasible in these various newspaper articles are not possible in the act of reading as here defined, but must be characteristic of such performance as skimming or scanning, in which relatively large portions of the reading material are skipped."

Comprehension, as previously defined, is difficult to measure literally. Most of the tests given on a speed-reading examination are to test retention of various facts in the article rather than understanding of principles and main ideas.

Real comprehension involves in most cases the complex approach taken in serious studying. The information must first be understood, repeated, probably reflected upon, and finally woven into a meaningful pattern. Whether or not this can be done at a very rapid rate depends on the complexity of the reading material and the reader's intelligence and skill.

But approached from strictly the memory point of view, it pays to read with a purpose and develop a reading style ... in effect, different reading gears. Where comprehension and "permanent" memory are desired, you must read carefully and well. Recitation and note-taking are techniques which will keep your reading highly active.

Learning to read so that you can retain a greater percentage of the material is a fundamental step in developing an all-around efficient memory. The person who learns to read well has taken a big step toward developing an instant memory power.

Putting Reading Principles to Work

To put these principles in action, let's assume you must—say, for business reasons—remember the main points of the following article, "Thunder from a Clear Blue Sky." It deals with sonic booms, the loud noise created by jet aircraft travelling at supersonic speed (762 miles an hour at sea level).

First, preview the article. Read selected parts such as the lead or introduction; the topic or introductory sentences to each paragraph, and perhaps occasionally the summary sentence to longer paragraphs; and finally, the conclusion. The main idea in previewing is to read these selected parts of the piece fairly rapidly, but carefully. This will give you a bird's-eye view of what the article is about; at the same time, it should help you pose questions about sonic booms. What causes them? How much damage do they cause? What are the chances of winning a claim for sonic-boom damage? If you preview the article in 2 minutes or less, you will be skimming at a rate of well over 1,000 words a minute. It might be helpful to have someone time you, notifying you when your reading time is half up.

Thunder from a Clear Blue Sky

A sudden thunderlike explosion rocked Milwaukee on a cloudless day last year, and within minutes newspapers, police, and fire stations were besieged with calls from an alarmed citizenry.

Among other things, the uproar was reported as an attack from outer space, broken gas mains, burglaries, a bank-robbery explosion, rampant *Nike* missiles from installations around the city, and an airline crash (from a woman who *saw* a wheel fall from the doomed airliner).

Actually, it was none of these. The real culprit was a sonic boom, created by a Strategic Air Command bomber streaking on a simulated combat sortie at twice the speed of sound.

Milwaukee's reaction to its first boom was perhaps typical. So was the assessed damage—a single broken lamp which had been jiggled off a table. Unhappily, the damage is sometimes more extensive.

Booms Here to Stay

Regardless, the sonic boom is the latest in the medley of jet-age noises to assail the American ear, and it obviously is here to stay. If your town hasn't been belted by a sonic explosion, don't go away! Booms are created by faster-than-sound jet planes, and virtually every fighter and bomber joining the U.S. aerial armada today has supersonic capability. What's more, experts are still predicting that supersonic transports will be whisking passengers across the country in the not-too-distant future, dragging their booms behind them.

The services are striving heroically to minimize booms, and their scientists are eagerly exploring ways to eliminate them altogether. But for the foreseeable future, this jet-age noise is, in official Air Force parlance, "unavoidable."

"Despite common acceptance of the term, there is still wide misunderstanding of a sonic boom—what it is, what causes it, and what it can do," said an Air Force claims officer.

Many people, for example, still think that a boom is created only at the moment a plane breaks the sound barrier. Actually, the plane drags the boom behind it as long as it travels supersonically (about 762 mph at sea level).

As the jet plane crashes into the slower air molecules, waves of energy or sound trail off behind in the form of a huge cone, much as water does when struck by the bow of a boat. The cone, travelling at the speed of sound, crashes into the ground, literally with a boom. The boom cuts a swath from a few miles to 50 miles wide, depending on the size, speed, and altitude of the plane.

Elements Affect Boom

Temperature, wind, humidity, and terrain also affect the boom's intensity. Booms really plaster flat country but tend to break up in mountainous terrain. Moisture and clouds ordinarily absorb some of the boom's punch. Prevailing winds at various altitudes may have either effect.

Such factors vary daily, even hourly. Thus a supersonic plane can fly across the country on any given day and create a spectrum of booms—from a sharp boom to no sound at all!

Altitude seems to be the most telling factor. The Air Force says that a supersonic bomber flying at 40,000 feet creates a boom that sounds like distant thunder. At 30,000 feet, the aircraft's boom is said to sound like close-range thunder—and at 20,000 feet, like an explosion.

The thunder analogy may be slightly imperfect. "Actually, it is just like a cannon going off right in your backyard," wrote an irate South Bend woman. She further suggested that repeated doses of such "artillery" could lead to something akin to shell shock.

And unlike thunder, a sonic boom comes literally from a clear blue sky. "It is always startling," a claims officer said, "and the complete absence of fire, smoke, lightning, or any visual evidence of its occurrence makes it difficult to understand."

The airplane itself gives no tip-off. It is travelling faster than sound, and can't be heard until seconds after the boom hits—if at all.

Unusual Claims for Boom Damage

For these reasons, sonic booms are thought to pack a potent destructive punch. The military has received damage claims for booms that allegedly cracked a swimming pool, broke water lines, smashed TV tubes, blew out furnaces, split trees, broke car windows, collapsed brick walls, and caved in a mine. One woman said she was criminally assaulted when a boom jarred open her back door, permitting an intruder to enter.

Claims for personal injury have included a heart attack, traumatic strain of muscles and ligaments, broken ear drums, fractured legs, and aggravation of arthritis and pre-existing polio deformity.

International solace was felt for the French inkeeper who reported that a king-sized boom caused his wine racks to collapse, smashing 4,000 bottles of rare vintage wine. *C'est la vie!* And it probably would have been sacrilege to disbelieve the claim by four Milwaukee churches that booms caused their organs to play off key.

Animals Affected

Animals have had their share of grievances. "It shouldn't have happened to a dog," wrote a man who said his canine companion needed psychiatric care after a few months of booms. A sonic explosion purportedly caused a prize show dog to suffer a miscarriage. And it was back to the beat for a member of the Collingsville, Ill. police canine corps who became boom shy.

A boom is said to have caused one farmer's chickens to go on an egg-laying strike, and an Arkansan felt that his dog died from fulminating pneumonia, "precipitated by over-exertion when frightened by a boom." Finally, a sonic explosion was blamed for frightening female minks, who destroyed their young and were rendered sterile.

Perhaps the most original claim, however, came from a St. Louis golfer who sought $1.50 a week for green fees. It seems he was stroking a putt in a local championship tourney when a big boom shook the links. Now, he claims to have a "gotcha neurosis."

Most Claims for Glass

But most claims received by the Air Force and by jet manufacturers—and apparently the most legitimate—are for broken plate and glass windows. For example, a college claimed one of its dormitories sustained an estimated 374 broken window panes (and this has got to be an educated guess) from a single sonic explosion.

Though the public complains vehemently now and then about sonic booms, formal claims against the U.S. government still haven't been excessive. Business, however, is picking up. The Air Force processed only 36 claims in 1956, compared to 6,481 claims in 1962. It paid off on only 2,990—or 46% of all claims submitted. Dollar-wise, payments came to $291,604.51, only 11.9% of the total value of claims turned in.

This means there's less than a 50-50 chance of your claim being approved. If it is approved, you'll likely receive only a little over one-tenth of the amount you claim.

Three Types of Claims

Does this sizable rejection rate indicate that a goodly number of citizens are looking for a home-repair at Uncle Sam's expense? Not necessarily. Claimants usually fall into three categories, according to H. Zonars, veteran aeronautical engineer at Wright-Patterson Air Force Base.

"Some people actually suffer damage," he says, "and some try to get the government to replaster a house that needed it before jets were around. Finally, there are those who sincerely believe the booms caused damage, although they did not."

The government bases its claims policy on a series of tests which shows that *a sonic boom created by one of its supersonic planes normally cannot injure a person or cause structural damage.* Test results indicate that booms *will* break glass that is improperly installed or under great tension, and in some cases aggravate existing plaster cracks. Bric-a-brac may be shaken from shelves.

On the basis of these findings, many of the foregoing claims were summarily dismissed.

Boom Measured in Overpressure

The explosion created by a sonic boom is measured in overpressure. Zonars' findings, which are often used as a rule-of-thumb index by Naval claimsmen, indicate that damage to a 4 x 6-foot window glass could start as low as 3.5 pounds of overpressure per square foot. Damage to a 3 x 4-foot window could start at 11 pounds of overpressure; plaster damage in a wood frame building at 14.3 pounds; wooden door damage at 20 pounds; and plaster damage in a concrete block building at 24.1 pounds of pressure.

How does this stack up with overpressures caused by jets? Well, normally, the Air Force claims, its planes will not create booms of over 5 pounds of overpressure. One bomber, for example, is said to cause overpressure of 1 pound per square foot at 40,000 feet; 2 pounds at 30,000 feet; and 3 pounds at 20,000 feet—under optimum conditions. But all jets, it is important to note, are usually under strict orders to make supersonic runs above 35,000 feet.

"The only supersonic flights made below 35,000 feet by a military bomber are over the Gulf of Mexico," a jet manufacturer said. "About the only damage they could do there is to give some fisherman a bigger bang out of the sport than he bargained for."

Damage to Building

What kind of overpressure is required to damage a brick or frame building? About 70 pounds, the military asserts. They hasten to add that the biggest boom made to date was 33 pounds of overpressure, made by a fighter flying supersonically 300 feet above a measuring device atop a mountain. But in the light of recent classified tests—and at least one incident—the 70-pound estimate may be in for a re-evaluation.

The incident occurred Nov. 4, 1959, on a cold, clear day. A fighter plane zoomed in over the nearly completed Uplands Airport at Ottawa, Canada at virtual tree-top level. The screaming jet accidentally slipped beyond the speed of sound, and a resounding boom crashed into the terminal building, subjecting it to five times the hurricane force it was built to withstand.

"One of the major items of damage was the twisting of metal window frames, particularly on the side of the building from which the aircraft was approaching," said John de Bondt of Canada's Department of Transport. "As a result, windows could not be closed as a great deal of replacement was necessary." Insulation was badly damaged.

Total damage to the terminal building came to $293,332, delaying the opening for months. Other structures in the vicinity were also damaged.

The Canadian incident might well have been the biggest and most costly boom claim to date. Certainly it dwarfs the largest claim paid by the U.S. Air Force, a $1,926.18 judgment to Jones Equipment Co. in Cedar City, Utah. The biggest claim turned in—for $19 million—was rejected hastily as having no basis.

Claimants Treated Fairly

A vast majority of claims, however, are neither as sensational nor as easy to adjudge. And despite the present hard policy on claims payments, military claimsmen, very often lawyers, bend over backward to see that the government plays fair with its complaining public.

In investigating a claim, the first step is to check all bases in the area of an alleged boom; this is done to determine if aircraft capable of creating booms routinely operate there. "To receive a claim, accompanied by irrefutable evidence that a sonic boom did in fact occur, and yet obtain reports from all military sources in the area denying presence of supersonic aircraft in the area, is highly frustrating," says Capt. G.A. Burwell, assistant director of litigation and claims for the U.S. Navy.

Yet, the military concedes that for a couple of good reasons this could happen. First, bases destroy their records every few months. Second, it could have been a *stray* boom, created by a pilot who went supersonically without realizing it (as in the Canadian case), or who unknowingly veered from his course.

For these reasons, the military isn't overly squeamish in every case about pinning down the specific plane that created the boom, nor do they demand admission from the pilot. One must surmise, however, that isolated boom claims would be suspect.

Once it's established that a military or manufacturer's jet could have caused a sonic boom, it must be determined that the boom did, in fact, cause the damage.

Glass Damage Is Tip-Off

First, the investigator looks for the existence—or absence—of glass damage, and whether similar damage from this incident has been verified in the area.

"Glass is the weakest element in a conventional structure," one officer said. "With very few exceptions, if there is any sonic boom damage, there should be broken glass."

"Ninety per cent of claims for cracks in walls are, in fact, old cracks that have gone unnoticed," he said. "Sonic booms won't cause new cracks, but they occasionally aggravate old ones." The engineer's report, age and condition of the building, and absence of other plaster complaints in the area are studied.

Why compare a damaged structure with other similar structures in the area? Because sonic booms usually aren't selective. For all practical purposes, overpressure should be the same over a fairly wide area. Why would a boom damage one house and not another, claimsmen ask logically, unless the damaged house was either too old or structurally weak. It often takes a structural engineer to answer this important question.

Structural Damage Denied

Structural damage, which is categorically denied by the military, is said to be caused almost invariably by faulty foundation, shifting of soil, improper design, alteration to structure resulting in weakening of load-bearing walls, or normal deterioration due to age.

Occurrences or absence of seismic disturbances in the locality, and other potential sources of damage, such as heavy trucks, rail traffic, or explosions, are also considered.

Now that you've completed the second reading, make notes of the facts which you feel *you* must retain for adequate comprehension. Do this before reading further. If you can't recall a fact, look it up hurriedly, then make notes. This is called post-viewing and it is tantamount to a "test."

The notes you made are no doubt slanted toward your specific needs. You filled in some details about the nature of booms and how they are affected by atmospheric conditions. You probably noted with interest, and perhaps some amusement, the several anecdotes, most of which you skimmed hurriedly the second time around. You undoubtedly jotted down some of the details about Zonars' rule-of-thumb findings about boom damage. And you no doubt noted some details about damage caused by low-flying jets.

Reading experts call this technique—previewing, reading thoroughly, and post-viewing—the multiple-reading method, and it embraces all of the principles of efficient memory. You have read with a purpose; you have used the sensory approach to learning by both writing facts down and reciting them; and you have used all-important repetition, enabling the information to jell in your memory.

Learning to read so that you can retain a great part of the material is a fundamental step in developing an all-around efficient memory. The person who learns to read well has taken a big step toward developing instant memory power.

Adding to Your Instant Memory Power Through Mnemonics-- Shorthand of the Mind (For Facts and Dates)

8

The term mnemonics stems from Mnemosyne, the Greek goddess of memory. A mnemonic technique is essentially an artificial memory device. The principle was illustrated in Chapter 5, when you used ten words as visual substitutes for numbers in remembering a list of "assignments."

These words are often called key words, because they are based on the *key-word alphabet* developed by the Germans many years ago. In this alphabet, numbers 0 through 9 are represented by various consonant sounds. Thus the alphabet can be used as a sort of mental shorthand to remember numbers. And it can also be used effectively as a basis for forming key words or word substitutes for numbers.

In the next few chapters, we'll use proven

memory techniques that will help you remember abstract facts and figures, unrelated facts, and, finally, names and faces. Put these techniques in perspective. They're not intended as a panacea for a poor memory. But these techniques will give you a method for remembering those pesky abstract things. For this reason alone, mnemonics is worth its weight in neurons. And once you have learned to cope better with the abstract, you're on your way to instant memory power.

The "Shorthand" Memory Alphabet

Here's the alphabet:

1	2	3	4	5	6	7	8	9	0
T	N	M	R	L	J	K	F	P	S
D					SH	Hard G	V	B	Z
TH					CH	Hard C	PH		Soft C
					Soft G	NG			
					TCH	Q			
					DG				

Vowels (*a, e, i, o, u,*) have no count in the alphabet; neither do *w, h,* and *y.* The letter *x,* for all practical purposes, counts as 70, since the system is based on sound or phonetics.

Like shorthand, the alphabet must be used over a period of time before it can be used effectively. However, here's a rule-of-thumb method which may help you remember the alphabet quicker. It goes like this:

The number 1 is represented basically by the *T* sound, since the *T* has one downstroke; 2 for *N,* since it has two downstrokes; 3 for *M,* three downstrokes; 4 for *R,* last letter in word fou*r*; 5 for *L,* Roman numeral for 50; 6 for *J,* looks like a backward 6; 7 for *K,* 7 comes 11; 8 for *f* (lower case) since both have a loop above and a loop below the line; 9 for *P,* backward 9; and 0 for *Z,* last letter in the alphabet.

Adding to Your Instant Memory Power Through Mnemonics   87

As a familiarization exercise, convert the following words into numbers: memory, girl, football, jet, children, rocket, elephant, rose.

Your answers should be: *MeMoRy*, 334; *GiRL*, 745; *FooT-BaLL*, 81955 (or a single 5); *JeT*, 61; *CHiLDReN*, 65142; *RoCKeT*, 471; *eLePHaNT*, 5821; and *RoSe*, 40. Practice a few more words until you get the "feel" of the alphabet and the phonetic arrangement.

Basically, the alphabet serves two purposes. It is a solid basis for forming key words, and it can be used, once mastered, to convert meaningless numbers into meaningful words. First, the key words.

In Chapter 5, you used key-word substitutes for numbers 1 through 10. In each case, the word was arbitrarily begun with an *h* and was followed by a vowel, neither of which had numerical value. Then, in each instance, the word ended with a consonant which corresponded to its place in the alphabet, 1 for *T*, 2 for *N*, and so forth.

Further, the key words represented objects which easily created a mental picture in your mind's eye—*hat, hen, ham*. Generally, verbs and adjectives—such as *hit* and *bad*—are not used, since they often do not create an easy-to-recall mental picture. The reason is that in such cases, you must visualize something being *hit* or something which is *bad,* instead of visualizing the object directly.

Forming Memorable Key Words

Two other factors should be considered when forming a key word. A mental picture with *action* in it is generally easier to remember than one in which the object is static. Your ability to remember the picture is further enhanced by its *vividness.* Something unusual in nature, especially if it's comical, is generally easier to remember than the commonplace. Therefore, words which lend themselves to one or both of these elements might make stronger key words.

In forming key words 10 through 19, you know that each word will begin with either a *T* or *D* and end in a consonant based on the alphabet, and in each case there is an intervening vowel.

Thus T — — S can represent a number of words, but probably only a couple will fit into the suggested format. *ToeS* is the logical choice, and you should again create a specific mental picture for the word. Similarly, the logical candidates for the other numbers in this series become: 11. *ToT;* 12. *TiN;* 13. *TeaM;* 14. *TiRe;* 15. *TiLL;* 16. *TiSHue;* 17. *TaCK;* 18. *TaFFy;* and 19. *TaPe.*

After forming the key words, use them in a trial run. Every person will make associations based on his own personal experiences. Thus every person will associate a little differently. The main guideline in establishing the key word is, "Does it work?"

The mnemonic technique, in any case, is based on your being totally familiar, visually speaking, with the key word. Ideally, you should be so familiar with the key word that when the number is mentioned, the visual substitute snaps on immediately in your mind's eye. You then simply associate the new object with the existing one in an interesting way. Ideally, again, the new object should be associated with the *fixed* key word, which is the *known* element. Since you use the same key word for the number each time, it pays to make the mental picture as "permanent" as possible in your imagination. The key word will work more effectively, of course, after you have used it often enough to know it intimately.

With these ideas in mind, review the newly learned key words carefully. In each case, create a specific visual image of the object so that it will reappear in the same form when the number is mentioned again.

Remembering Sales Features

Let's use the words in an exercise. Assume you are a representative of an aluminum foil company and want to remember—in a hurry—ten summertime uses of your product. As you review each item, associate it with the number.

The first use of aluminum will be to wrap shoes, cosmetics, and face powder in foil, and to interleaf suits and dresses to keep them from wrinkling before packing. Number 10 is *ToeS*. In this case,

Adding to Your Instant Memory Power Through Mnemonics 89

visualize your mental picture, the key word. Now, with your *ToeS* in action, have them going through these various steps of wrapping items in foil. The other sales points are:

11. Placing wrapping under a sleeping bag insulates against dampness. Visualize your *ToT* spreading foil on the baby crib (or whatever), then stretching out for a little nap.

12. Parking bicycle outdoors. Use foil over the bicycle seat to protect it. Visualize water pouring from your *TiN* cup onto the bicycle seat, which of course, is covered.

13. Use for cooking. Have your *TeaM* fashioning skillets and other utensils from the foil and perhaps cooking a meal.

14. Cover snacks. Wrap a sandwich in foil, place it in your freezer, and insert in your *TiRe*. It'll be there, hopefully, when you revisit the scene visually in a moment.

15. For baby care. If you have to camp out, place a couple of long strips between the sheet and mattress—a good substitute for a waterproof pad. Carrying out this act in your *TiLL* creates an amusing and vivid scene.

16. Emergency signal. If you run out of gas or your battery goes dead, strip the side of your car with foil, which will reflect light from oncoming headlights. Use your *TiSHue* to polish the siding visually.

17. For ironing. Foil is a good "rest" for your electric iron. So *TaCK* the iron onto your board as a reminder.

18. Kneeling pad. If you have to change a flat or work on the ground, aluminum makes a nice pad. Visualize yourself fixing a flat near your *TaFFy*.

19. Cool it. Wrap ice cubes in foil for extra protection. Do it with your *TaPe* to measure just how cool it is.

Now try to recall the ten sales points, using key words 10 through 19.

Again, key words must be used by the individual to test their workability. As a final exercise in this area, here are some suggested key words for numbers 20 through 29. Use them to remember the following grocery list of ten items: lemon pie, eggs, carrots, salt, frankfurters, bread, apples, coffee, bananas, and a mop.

20. Slam your *lemon pie* into your *NoSe*. It's pure slapstick, but creates a vivid, action-packed, and hopefully highly memorable mental picture.

21. *NeT* (perhaps a tennis net) is the key word. Bombard the *NeT* with *eggs* instead of tennis balls. It could be a rotten-egg sight.

22. Visualize your *NuN* noisily crunching *carrots* where it'll be noticed most—during prayer services.

23. Pour *salt* freely over the city of *NoMe*. Remember, it's not snowing, but *salt*ing in *NoMe*.

24. Have *NeRo* chowing down on a slightly unregal fare of *frankfurters*, or have him roasting *franks*.

25. Picture yourself trying unsuccessfully to drive a *NaiL* through your "no-so-fresh" *bread*.

26. *NaSH* is the key word; fill it with several basketsful of delicious red *apples*.

27. In your favorite *NooK*, place an oversized *coffee* pot and pour freely.

28. *NaVy* is the key word. Whatever your mental picture, add enough *bananas* to float a battleship.

29. Visualize yourself using a *mop* to clean and polish the key word, *NoB*.

If you want to go further with key words, here are some suggested items for 30 through 100: 30. Moss; 31. Mitt; 32. Mane; 33. Mom; 34. Mire; 35. Mail; 36. Match; 37. Mike; 38. Movie; 39. Map; 40. Rose; 41. Rat; 42. Rain; 43. Ram; 44. Rare; 45. Rail; 46. Rash; 47. Rock; 48. Roof; 49. Rope; 50. Lease; 51. Light; 52. Lion; 53. Lime; 54. Lair; 55. Lil; 56. Leash; 57. Lock; 58. Leaf; 59. Lap; 60. Joes; 61. Jet; 62. June; 63. Jam; 64. Jury; 65. Jail; 66. Judge; 67. Jockey; 68. Joseph; 69. Jap.

Also, 70. Cows; 71. Kite; 72. Can; 73. Camel; 74. Cur; 75. Call; 76. Cage; 77. Cook; 78. Cuff; 79. Cape; 80. Foes; 81. Fat; 82. Fan; 83. Foam; 84. Fire; 85. Foil; 86. Fish; 87. Fake; 88. Fife; 89. Fop;

Adding to Your Instant Memory Power Through Mnemonics 91

90. Posse; 91. Pot; 92. Pen; 93. Puma; 94. Pier; 95. Pail; 96. Page; 97. Pick; 98. Puff; 99. Pope; 100. Daisies.

You can use a limited number of your key words to recall key ideas in short speeches, the main points of a sales pitch, or any number of totally unrelated facts in sequence. Or, you can really surprise your friends by learning enough key words to "memorize" an entire magazine. You do this simply by associating the main idea or object on the page with the appropriate key word. But now, let's use the key-word alphabet to remember numbers.

You may be one of those rare individuals blessed with a natural ability to remember numbers. Consider yourself extremely fortunate and decidedly in the minority. Unless a number has some special significance—and few longer-digit numbers do—it poses a formidable memory problem.

Learning Numbers in "Parts"

One of the "natural" methods for remembering numbers involves learning them in "parts" rather than as a whole. For example, you generally remember a telephone number by repeating it in segments: Whitehall 1-2941, would be recalled as (Wh-1) (29) (41). Learning smaller individual units is easier than trying to retain the longer number.

You can sometimes associate numbers artificially. In the above case, for example, you might remember yourself as "No. 1." Then cite '29 as the year of the stock market crash, and '41 as the year in which World War II started for the United States.

Another often-used system is to break a longer number into more meaningful parts—for example, 149212365201969. Impossible to remember? Not if you break it into parts and remember 1492 (Columbus discovered America), 12,365 (height of Mt. Fuji), and July 20, 1969 (man landed on the moon). Simple? Hardly! And for precisely this reason, such systems are usually effective only in dire emergencies. In the first place, most longer-digit numbers would not work out so conveniently. In the second place, it would be difficult to remember that many "stories" for any series of longer-digit numbers. True, you would have given the number some meaning, but probably only tentatively.

Remembering Phone Numbers

The key-word alphabet provides the most logical (although not infallible) method, since it provides a system for converting meaningless numbers into meaningful words. Using the systems for telephone numbers is a case in point.

The telephone exchange can be included in the conversion. Or, preferably, it can be omitted in most cases, since this is a "known" factor. In your own city, you probably routinely associate various sections with the various exchanges. In such cases, including the exchange in the transposition would be superfluous memory work.

Being able to convert numbers successfully into words hinges on two factors. First, you must know the system well enough to use the various combinations offered by the alphabet; second, you must use considerable creative imagination. The more meaningful you can make the words, and couple them with a meaningful and vivid mental picture, the more likely you are to remember the number.

Here are a few examples of telephone numbers of various students, based on what little information was available at the time about them. Mr. Ashmore was an accountant. His telephone number: PE 7-9076. Translated, this becomes:

	K	ee	P	S	C	a	SH
PE	7	-	9	0	7		6

This word combination, under the circumstances, should be relatively easy to remember. But it appears "easy" to form only after the fact. These numbers could have been converted into any number of word combinations. The more meaning, however, the easier the words are to remember.

The idea is to link the words to some known fact about the person, thus enabling the laws of association to work for you more effectively. Here is the telephone number of a Mr. Grubis: MA

Adding to Your Instant Memory Power Through Mnemonics

4-4851. Without knowing any more about the person than this, the assignment is difficult. Now you learn that he is in the wholesale meat business (another coincidence), and you automatically absorb this fact into your decision-making apparatus. This made me evolve the combination:

	R	a	R	e	F	i	L	e	T
MA	4	-	4		8		5		1

Then, there's the pediatrician whose number came out:

	C	u	Re	Li'	L	Boys
PE	7	-	4	5	5	9

In this case, a variation of spelling can often be remembered more easily than the standard spelling. The same idea is true in this number—a woman who prided herself for having once lived on a farm:

	CH	u	R	N		
ED	6	-	4	2	2	2

Then there is the case of the fire chief whose number came out:

	C	o	Me	R	u	N	i	N'
PE	7	-	3	4		2		2

The only rigid requirement is that the numbers be in succession. The final word can use any number of letters, as in the case of this lawyer's number:

	Ri		CH	M	aN	Lawyer
AT	4	-	6	3	2	5

Remembering Code Numbers

You can use the alphabet similarly to convert any series of numbers—except perhaps a very long series of numbers—into meaningful words. For the most part, you would likely use the system where you need to remember many numbers or lengthy codes. For example, remembering all the number codes in the library's Dewey classification system would be virtually impossible. However, remembering an appreciable number of the class-

94   Adding to Your Instant Memory Power Through Mnemonics

ifications might be made easier by converting the number for a subject into words. The more relevant the words, the easier they are to remember. And, of course, visualization—especially a vivid mental picture—might help you in the assignment. As an example, here are a few conversions for random topics:

Subject	Classification Number
Adventure and Travel	BoaT S o Re 9 1 0. 4 (picture yourself on a deck chair)
Naval history WW II	Pu R Se R Loafs (a real eight- 9 4 0. 4 5 ball)
Recreation accident statistics	Ma De New Ru Les (after 3 1 2. 4 5 the accidents, of course)
Memory aids	TaiLo R e D (to meet the situation, 1 5 4. 1 naturally)
Lumber building construction material	CHoP iT THick 6 9 1. 1
Men's Christian Societies	uN SHaK e N 2 6 7. 2
War crimes international	Mu R D e R 3 4 1. 4
Algebra	Pi CKuP Fast 9 7 9. 8
African violets	L oVe My Fragrance 5 8 3. 8
Spies WW II	P RieS a Re Va Luable 9 4 0. 4 8 5

Familiarity with the key-word alphabet is the key to forming effective word conversions. Like shorthand, the alphabet must be used a little every day if you hope to master it.

As you've no doubt already surmised, the alphabet can be used to convert price lists, estimates, financial statements—in short,

Adding to Your Instant Memory Power Through Mnemonics

virtually any series of numbers—into meaningful representative words, though some ingenuity is generally required.

For example, here's how one engineer used the alphabet to remember, where needed, the square root to the fourth figure of numbers 2 through 10:

Number	Square Root	Association
2.	1.414	RaT Race. Visualize two rats running a race. Obviously, the digit for the first number is known and needs no conversion.
3.	1.732	KiMoNo. Picture a kimono covered with triangles, symbolic of three.
5.	2.236	eNMeSH. Visualize the five-sided pentagon enmeshed in red tape.
6.	2.449	RaRe Bee. Six suggests a hexagonal shape, perhaps a beehive. A multi-headed bee could be a rare one.
7.	2.645	SHeeR Linen. Seven suggests dice or a dance of seven veils, done with sheer linen.
8.	2.828	FuNNy Face. How about "ate" for eight, and a funny face after taking a bite.
10.	3.162	TouCH Nose. You have ten fingers. Touch your toes with them.

Learning to master the memorization of numbers advances you another big step toward that instant memory power. Few boast real proficiency in this difficult area.

Doubling Your Instant Memory Power with an Alternate Channel

9

How many key words will you need to master? It depends entirely on your needs. If you must routinely remember long lists of disconnected facts, you can profitably learn several series of key words. The same holds true if you want to "memorize" a deck of cards or carry out other impressive mnemonic feats. Many, however, will find it expedient to master only a relatively few key words to use in remembering short series of disconnected facts. Or, with a little practice, you can use the key words to remember a sequence of ideas in a short speech or report.

Using Logical Extension

If you wish to master only a limited number of key words, there is a method inherent in the learning of key words themselves that will enable you to master an alternate key word for each basic word quite easily. Thus if you have ten usable key words, you can easily learn another ten based on them; if you can thoroughly learn 20 words, you can easily develop 20 alternates, giving you a total of 40 such words on which you can hang all sorts of things in your memory. The key word must create a firm, specific mental picture. Then this picture "triggers" a secondary mental picture (which associates itself with the key-word mental picture, but is distinctly different from it), leading to recall of the secondary key word.

Assuming you know your basic list of key words quite thoroughly, for example, you will respond to No. 1 by visualizing your *hat*. This mental response will become automatic and virtually instantaneous after you have practiced using the word a number of times. Now, the alternate key word is formed by visualizing an object which readily associates with *hat,* but which forms a *separate* mental picture. This alternate word must, of course, have meaning to *you.*

I use the word *rack* (a hat rack, naturally). The mental picture this creates is a *rack* used in an office, a visual picture which is clearly distinguishable from my regular *hat*. The distinction is necessary to avoid confusion in remembering two separate items with No. 1.

Switching Memory Channels

For example, assume you have used your basic No. 1 key word, *hat,* for remembering a list of assignments. At the same time, you wish to use No. 1 again to remember, say, the first main point in a report or speech. In this case, No. 1 triggers your basic key word, *hat,* which you know is already in use. Immediately, you mentally switch over to another "channel," and you instantly visualize your alternate key word, *rack*.

Although seemingly quite involved, this process is relatively simple. Your ability to use the alternate list successfully will depend in large measure on how easily you can use your basic key words.

What makes an effective alternate key word? Only through trial-and-error can you tell. As a starter, you might use a word-association experiment. Simply list your ten to 20 basic key words, then quickly jot down the first thing that each word brings to mind. Sometimes this is the very word that will work. In other cases, the word will have to be dropped, since it does not lend itself to a distinctly separate mental picture.

Tentatively, you might try this list, forming in each case a separate mental picture:1. hat-rack; 2. hen-egg; 3. ham-pineapple; 4. hair-comb; 5. hill-top; 6. hedge-clippers; 7. hook-brook; 8. hive-honey; 9. hoop-barrel; 10. toes-boots.

Remembering a List of Regulations

After you've taken a few minutes to firm up a distinct mental picture for your alternate key word—one that can't be confused visually with the basic key word—try using your alternate list to "remember" this list of safety regulations.

In each case read the item for meaning, then repeat the gist or main idea in your own words. An idea, like an object, can be visualized readily if it is symbolized by a representative object. For example, the idea of "freedom" might be symbolized by several things: the Statue of Liberty, an American flag, broken handcuffs, or any number of visual cues. The symbolism that occurs to you is usually the one that will work best. In any case, your symbolism will be like a fingerprint—unique. With this in mind, review your alternate key words again so that you will be quite familiar with them. Now use these alternate words to remember ten safety regulations. To get the feel of the technique, perhaps you'll want to use the following association as a starter. Here are ten steps to remember:

1. *Horseplay, running, and practical jokes are not permitted on company property.*

No. 1 evokes your basic key word, *hat*. This time bypass the basic key word and switch to the alternate key word, *rack*. Next, pinpoint the main idea and translate it into a symbolic object which you can visualize. In this case, the main idea appears to be "no horseplay." Use a horse as a symbol and place him on the *rack*. Naturally, he'll be stumbling or playing around, and you could be kidding him about it. Thus the mental picture of the horse *running* around the *rack* while playing with you is quite vivid and action-packed.

2. *Inform your supervisor if you have trouble with electrical equipment. He will call an electrician if needed.*

Your second alternate word is *egg*, in whatever form you wish. This one happens to be an *egg* container in the refrigerator. In this case, simply visualize yourself inserting an electrical plug, not into a regular outlet, but into the *egg*. The "yolk," of course, will be on you.

3. *Protective equipment, such as respirators, hard hats, and rubber or asbestos gloves, are furnished by the company and must be worn on jobs requiring this type of protection.*

Protection is the main idea, and it can be readily symbolized by some of the objects mentioned, plus others which may be more meaningful to you. *Pineapple* is the alternate word; mentally drape it with a hard hat (which you might bang on a couple of times for action's sake). The *pineapple* would look even funnier with rubber gloves and a respirator on it.

4. *Be sure materials are not stored or piled so as to block fire extinguishers, safety valves, sprinkler heads, fire-alarm boxes, or emergency equipment.*

How about visualizing a workman piling boxes on your oversized *comb*. For a vivid picture with action, visualize yourself saturating the material with a nearby fire extinguisher. Then to complete the visual story, picture your overhead sprinkler system putting out the fire.

5. *Use compressed air only on work functions requiring its use. It is not to be used for cleaning clothes or hands, benches, floors, or released close to the body of yourself or a fellow worker.*

A mental picture of air jetting from a compressor affords plenty of action. The alternate word is a *top*. Literally spin the *top* around with the compressor. For good measure, visualize a shirt over the *top*. Remember, air is not to be used to clean clothing.

6. *Loose or torn clothing, ties, open cuffs, must not be worn*

Doubling Your Instant Memory Power with an Alternate Channel   101

around moving machinery. Jewelry may not be worn around moving machinery, or if your job requires working with electrical circuits or climbing.

Clippers is the alternate word. Immediately inject into the mental picture a machinist at work. Now start clipping away at the workman's trousers, then his shirt, then his rings and watch. When you think of No. 6, in a few seconds the picture should come back to you—then the main idea.

7. *Report all plant injuries, regardless of severity, to your supervisor or to the nearest first-aid station—immediately! Never attempt self-treatment. A slight injury may become infected if not properly treated.*

"Injury" or "first aid" is the main idea here. Symbolize the idea with either a Red Cross ambulance or perhaps a man on crutches. Whatever you select, have it floating down your *brook,* your alternate key word for No. 7. Another helpful idea might be to place a doctor in the scene.

8. *Safety glasses or other approved eye protection are furnished by the company and must be worn at all times when grinding, sawing, drilling, or chipping. You may purchase safety glasses ground to your prescription at the tool service store.*

Visualize your alternate word, *honey.* Pour the *honey* over your glasses and you find yourself in a real safety dilemma; you can't see at all. This should serve as a vivid reminder to wear safety glasses at all times.

9. *Women must wear approved hair covering when working around revolving machinery or equipment.*

Barrel is the alternate key word. Visualize a lady in your *barrel* (perhaps this is her only attire), and have her working near machinery. Throw a king-sized net over her hair, and the big *barrel* to boot. This way, you can hardly forget the main idea—a cover for women's hair when working near machinery.

10. *It is a poor practice to pile or leave tools or loose material on ladders, stairs, stands, or scaffolding.*

Place your alternate key-word picture, *boots,* on any of the above items. Now have the *boots* themselves doing a Mexican hat dance, stomping on all sorts of tools and delicate equipment which shouldn't be there in the first place.

The exercise is over. Now try mentally reviewing your list. In each case, the number should conjure a picture of your basic key word, which should in turn "turn on" the alternate word. The alternate word will hopefully lead you to the main point you want to remember.

An important point to keep in mind is that you did not "memorize" the report with key words. You learned the report through meaningful reading and repetition, then used your key words as pegs for your outline. Try it on that next extemporaneous speech or report.

Whenever the basic key words are "occupied," the alternate list can be switched on and used quite effectively. Having alternate words is an easy way to get "two words for one."

Remembering Playing Cards

With practice, you can learn to use the alternate list of key words in several different ways. Probably one of the most ingenious feats is to use key words to remember playing cards—or even an entire deck of cards. Actually, the system would probably be advantageous only to the extreme card buff. Or, it can be turned into an impressive parlor feat. In the system, each card is assigned a specific number:

	Clubs	Diamonds	Hearts	Spades
Ace	11	21	31	41
2	12	22	32	42
3	13	23	33	43
4	14	24	34	44
5	15	25	35	45
6	16	26	36	46
7	17	27	37	47
8	18	28	38	48
9	19	29	39	49
10	10	20	30	40

Doubling Your Instant Memory Power with an Alternate Channel

	Clubs	Diamonds	Hearts	Spades
Jack	61	71	81	91
Queen	62	72	82	92
King	63	73	83	93

Each suit is represented by a series of numbers for easy identification (clubs, teens; diamonds, 20s; hearts, 30s; and spades, 40s). A system similar to the one shown must be adopted for face cards. Here, too, uniformity is important for quick identification.

Assume the following four players have played these cards and you wish to make note of the fact.

Mr. Smith, 7 of clubs. Clubs is the teen series, making the card 17 on *tack*. Visualize Mr. Smith sitting on the *tack*. The sight is almost enough to break up the game.

Mrs. Brown, 2 of diamonds. The key word is 22 or *nun*. Visualize the *nun* and Mrs. Brown engaged in a lively discussion over playing cards.

Mr. Wagner, 6 of hearts. The key word for 36 is *match*. Visualize Mr. Wagner getting "burned" as a result of playing his cards poorly. The idea is to give him a visual hot-foot.

Mrs. Jones, 9 of spades. The key word is 49, or *rope*. Visually lasso Mrs. Jones and don't forget she's now "roped in."

You can learn to remember a deck of cards in sequence as a parlor trick, too, if you're willing to put in the considerable time and effort required. The feat also demands considerable concentration. To perform this act, you need to "know" the designations for the 52 playing cards, as shown in the chart. The alternate key words are used to follow the sequence of cards; the regular basic key words are used to identify the cards. Assuming the first five cards shown are as follows, here's the method of identification:

No. 1, alternate key word is *rack*. The first playing card is the 9 of hearts or *map*. Simply visualize your *map* spinning around on your *rack*.

No. 2 card is the 5 of spades. The alternate key word is *egg;* the playing card is *rail.* Visualize your *egg* riding the *rail*.

No. 3 card is 10 of clubs. In this case, have your *toes* dipping into your third alternate key word, *pineapple*.

No. 4 is the 4 of diamonds. Alternate key word is *comb*, which you must visualize with 24, *Nero*.

And No. 5 is the ace of clubs, No. 11. Associate your *tot* with the alternate key word for 5, *top*. An interesting mental picture!

To perform such a feat, you'll naturally need alternate key words through 52. And you'll have to concentrate on "all four burners." In fact, even if you don't want to memorize an entire deck of cards, you can still use the technique to a lesser degree to practice extending your concentration span.

But if you do elect to try the feat—and succeed—there's no doubt about it. You're on your way to a genuine instant memory.

Using Instant Memory Power to Create a Mental Calendar   10

Fortunately, except for birthdays and anniversaries, most of us don't feel compelled to remember a great number of dates. Were we required to do so, most of us would find the job exceedingly difficult. Dates, from a pure memory standpoint, have little meaning and thus fall into the abstract and hard-to-remember category.

Should you need to remember rather long lists of dates, however, there is a mnemonic technique which can help. Essentially, the technique involves giving the date "meaning" by converting the numbers into relevant words. The extra mnemonic step in remembering dates is to add a visual picture code for the month. Those symbols used were selected for obvious reasons. Others will probably work better for you if they are personalized. Tentatively, however, you might give the pictures below a trial run.

Months as Pictures

Picture January as a new year's baby; February as George Washington; March, as a "wind man";

April, as showers; May, as a Maypole; June, as a bride; July, as a skyrocket; August, as Caesar; September, as a schoolhouse; October, as an octopus; November, as a Pilgrim; and December, as Santa Claus.

To memorize a date, the first step is to convert the numbers into words. For example, let's take the date on which the Japanese surrendered to General MacArthur. The armistice was signed aboard the battleship *Missouri* Sept. 2, 1945. Since you know—and need not necessarily "remember"—that the signing took place in the 1900s, all that needs converting are the date and the last two digits of the year:

	New		Ru		Le
Sept.	2,	1	9	4	5

"New Rule" becomes your fairly-easy-to-remember word code. Now you must add the month. In remembering the occasion, you of course visualize General MacArthur signing the armistice aboard the battleship. In order to remember the month, inject into the mental picture a visual representation of the month, in this case the *schoolhouse*. The key elements to remember are the words, which should be made as meaningful as possible, and the visual symbol, indicating the month.

Or, let's assume you need to remember the date on which the *Lusitania* was sunk: May 7, 1915. Even though you are aware that the tragedy occurred in the 1900's, you might still want to use all of the numbers for the sake of convenience. It might work like this:

	Qui	T	Ba	T	Le
May	7,	1	9	1	5

There's a slight variation in spelling, of course, which should be easy to remember. The words QuiT BaTLe are significant in that the *Lusitania* had to do just that when it went down. You can visualize the sinking ship, along with the symbol for May—sinking maypole.

Using Instant Memory Power to Create a Mental Calendar 107

Remembering Earlier Historic Dates

In other cases, where you are not certain of the century, or where it is convenient to use all numbers, it is a good practice to do so. Here is the date of the end of the Siege of Vicksburg:

           Ru   SH Men
July 4,   1   8   6   3

or

       RaiD oF CHaMps
July 4, 1 8   6   3

It's quite easy to visualize soldiers assaulting Vicksburg, and to remember the words RuSH Men, or RaiD oF CHaMps. The month is "added" by visualizing your symbol for July, *skyrocket,* in place of artillery perhaps.

If the date is some time in the past, it might be necessary again to use the entire date in the conversion. For example, if you need to recall the date on which Joan of Arc was burned at Rouen, you might want to do it this way:

        My S   Te   Ry   MaiD
May 3   0,   1   4   3   1

Your visual picture will probably have Joan at the stake. Make it a maypole scene and you have quite an occasion—visually speaking. Remember, MySTeRy MaiD.

For good measure, here are a couple of other historical dates of more recent years. Hitler died in Berlin on April 30, 1945. Should you need to retain the date, here's a possibility:

         Mi S   Ru Le
April   3   0,   1   9   4   5

In this case, the century is known to virtually everyone. The word MiSRuLe becomes appropriate considering Hitler's life-style. You would simply visualize him in the bunker in Berlin amid softly falling April showers. Into each life some rain must fall, even Hitler's.

Or, let's take the date on which the Armistice was signed in World War I. It has many conversion possibilities, including:

        Da Te   TouGH
Nov. 1 1, 1 9 1 8

or maybe
DeaTH   Di Ve
Nov. 1 1, 1 9 1 8

Picture the signing in Paris, and the rather incongruous picture of a Pilgrim (representing November) along for the historic occasion. These words, or others, could serve as your reminder.

Remembering the Day of the Month

If you are called on frequently to recall a substantial number of dates, this system can serve you well. Speaking of dates, here's a mnemonic technique that falls largely into the fun-and-games category, although it might well come in handy during workaday business situations. The technique will enable you to figure out—rather quickly, once you've gotten the hang of it—the day of the week on which most dates fall. In this system, months and days of the week are given these numerical values:

Month	Value
June	0
September, December	1
April, July	2
January, October	3
May	4
August	5
February, March, November	6

Using Instant Memory Power to Create a Mental Calendar 109

Sunday counts 1; Monday 2; Tuesday 3; Wednesday 4; Thursday 5; Friday 6; and Saturday 0.

To figure the day of the week for dates from 1801 to 1900, add one-fourth of the final two digits of the year to the final two digits; add the number index for the month; add the day of the month; then divide by seven; the *remainder* will be the day of the month on which that date fell.

Here's how to use the formula to reckon the day on which October 5, 1888 fell: one-fourth of the last two digits (88) is 22; 22 plus 88 equals 110, adding the number for the month (3 for October) brings the total to 113; add the day of the month (October 5) and you raise the total to 118; now divide by 7 and you get a *remainder* of 6, which is Friday.

Let's try April 20, 1816. One-fourth of 16 is 4, which added to 16 gives you 20; add 2 for the month (April), giving you 22; add the day of the month (April 20) and you raise the total to 42; divide by 7 and you get *no* remainder; thus the day is 0, or Saturday.

Where the last two figures of the year cannot be divided by 4 exactly, *ignore the fraction*. Take October 21, 1805, for example: one-fourth of 5 is 1 (ignore the fraction); add this to the year for 6; add the number for October (3) and you have 9; 9 divided by 7 leaves a *remainder* of 2, which means October 21, 1805, was on a *Monday*.

The formula works differently for dates that fall between 1901 and 2000. All the steps are the same, except you must *deduct 2 from the total*.

Here's how this system works for March 12, 1937: one-fourth of 37 is 9 (ignore the fraction), which added to 37 equals 46; adding the count for March (6) and the day of the month (12), brings the total to 64; subtract 2 (for the 20th Century) and you get 62; divide 62 by 7 and you get a remainder of 6, which is *Friday*.

For October 21, 1906: one-fourth of 6 is 1 (ignore the fraction), which added to 6 equals 7; adding 3 for October and 21 for the day of the month pushes the total to 31; subtract 2 for the 20th Century and this leaves 29; divide by 7 and the *remainder* is 1, which is *Sunday*.

Remembering a Busy Schedule

So much for historical dates. Now let's get down to brass tacks about a busy schedule you're to follow on Monday. You'll have a daily list of activities to remember (using your basic key words), plus a speech to recall (using your alternate key words). It's a good example, hopefully, of how you can use relatively few key words, along with an alternate key word, to fullest advantage.

Here's your busy schedule for a Monday:

Time	Appointment
8 a.m.	Weekly breakfast with Lion's Club Breakfast Group
9 a.m.	Meet with Chamber of Commerce aviation committee
10 a.m.	Review your department's budget for the coming year
11 a.m.	Take care of your backlog of correspondence
12 noon	Speak before a luncheon held by City Safety Council
1 p.m.	Pick up airline tickets for trip to New York next week
2 p.m.	Interview applicants for executive post
3 p.m.	Present bonus award to company's top salesman of the month
4 p.m.	Appointment at dentist's office
5 p.m.	A game of tennis at the club
6 p.m.	It's your anniversary; don't forget to drop by the florist's and pick up a dozen roses on the way home
7 p.m.	Dinner at your favorite restaurant, followed by the theater, "Fiddler on the Roof."

The ten key points to that speech you're making at noon to the Safety Council are: 1. Stop—failure to do so may result in serious

Using Instant Memory Power to Create a Mental Calendar 111

criminal consequences. 2. Render first aid where necessary. 3. Protect the scene from further damage. 4. Call an officer. 5. Gather information about the accident. 6. Avoid making statements; be careful of what you say. 7. See your doctor. 8. Consult your lawyer immediately. 9. Inform your insurance company promptly. 10. Report the accident to the Department of Public Safety. These are only the main topic headings, of course. You have properly prepared by reading the details of each of these steps and capturing the meaning. All you need now is a cue to remind you of the proper sequence of steps.

Admittedly, this is a formidable memory workout: 12 appointments and ten key points to an "extemporaneous" speech. Here's how you might want to attack the problem, using only 12 basic key words and ten alternate key words.

First the appointments:

Time	Key Word	Association
8 a.m.	HIVE	HIVE is the basic key word. Visualize a group of LIONS—real ones, that is—attacking the bee HIVE, probably with humorous results.
9 a.m.	HOOP	Picture a 747 jumbo jet squeezing through your HOOP, to the delight of the applauding AVIATION COMMITTEE.
10 a.m.	TOES	BUDGET is the main idea; have your TOES scanning the ledger sheet, trying to get a TOE-hold on the net value.
11 a.m.	TOT	Put your TOT in the unusual position of typing away on your BACKLOG of letters.

Time	Key Word	Association
12 noon	TIN	SAFETY is the main idea here. Picture yourself orating magnificently in your TIN cup.
1 p.m.	HAT	Visualize an AIRPLANE circling your HAT; and don't forget to pick up the TICKETS.
2 p.m.	HEN	Put your HEN in the executive suite and have him INTERVIEWING prospective employees.
3 p.m.	HAM	Picture your top salesman HAMMING it up on your HAM, waving his cash AWARD BONUS.
4 p.m.	HAIR	This one should be easy to get your teeth into, with the DENTIST fighting through your shaggy HAIR to get the tooth.
5 p.m.	HILL	Visualize your favorite HILL, and picture yourself executing a tennis forehand smash.
6 p.m.	HEDGE	Roses don't normally grow in a HEDGE, but they do this time; oversized ones, of course, for your anniversary.
7 p.m.	HOOK	Picture a "FIDDLER" on your HOOK, playing while you enjoy your anniversary dinner.

Using Instant Memory Power to Create a Mental Calendar

Speaking Without Notes

So much for the list of appointments; now for that speech. Since you've already used your basic key words, switch channels and use your alternate key words for remembering the ten basic ideas of your talk. Since you're going to associate with ideas rather than objects, you'll have to select, in each case, a symbol which represents the idea, like this:

Number	Alternate Word	Association
1	RACK	How about a STOP SIGN or something familiar to you spinning around on your RACK.
2	EGG	FIRST AID is the idea. It's a ridiculous picture, but visualize yourself applying a tourniquet to an EGG.
3	PINEAPPLE	A FLARE might depict the "protection" idea. Naturally you'll stick the flare in your alternate word, PINEAPPLE.
4	COMB	Visually contact an OFFICER, and for memory's sake, have him COMBing his hair.
5	TOP	Gathering facts is the idea, symbolized perhaps by a REPORTER spinning furiously on your TOP.
6	CLIPPERS	How about placing a BAND AID over your mouth, or use a HUSH gesture to symbolize

Number	Alternate Word	Association
		the idea of caution in speech. Use your CLIPPERS to cut the band-aid away.
7	BROOK	See your DOCTOR swimming upstream in a BROOK while giving a physical.
8	HONEY	Picture your LAWYER in the HONEY, and you might want to throw in a little sweet talk, too.
9	BARREL	INSURANCE salesmen have literally got you over the BARREL, visually speaking. Remember, the main idea: to contact your own insurance company.
10	BOOTS	Picture the emblem for your DEPARTMENT OF PUBLIC SAFETY; now visually use your BOOTS to help "stamp in" safety if the damage is over $25.

Once you've mastered these techniques, you'll be able to perform a memory feat few can duplicate: remember, mentally set up your own "mental calendar." It's a hazardous mission, and only those with instant memory power need apply.

11

Using Instant Memory Power to Master Hard-to-Recall Facts

> In fourteen hundred ninety-two
> Columbus sailed the ocean blue.

Odds are you remember—and likely will never forget—this catchy little ditty you learned as a child. Reason: it has meaning. The date itself, on the other hand, is just another abstract number.

Few, for example, probably recall outright that Paul Revere made his famous ride on April 18, 1775. But it's not difficult to find a person who can recite:

> Listen my children and you will hear,
> Of the midnight ride of Paul Revere.
> On the eighteenth of April in Seventy-Five,
> Hardly a man is now alive
> Who remembers that famous day and year ...

And some might recall that:

> William the Fourth, he went to heaven,
> In eighteen hundred and thirty-seven.

Most of us start acquiring such memory crutches early in life and continue to garner them throughout our adult life. And why not? A crutch can frequently ease the load on our overburdened memory.

As a youngster, for example, you probably learned, and still remember that it's:

> I before E
> Except after C
> Or when sounded as A
> As in neighbor and weigh.

And then there was the old man river, the Mississippi, otherwise known as:

> M - I
> Crooked letter, crooked letter
> I
> Crooked letter, crooked letter
> I
> Hump back, hump back
> I

Later you might have learned the difference between principle and principal by remembering that the latter is a *pal* to you. Get it? If you did, you won't forget it.

Secretarial Spelling Crutches

Secretaries are frequently known for their ingenuity in creating spelling crutches. After all, it can save a number of frantic excursions to the dictionary. How, for example, do you spell the "stuff" you write letters on, with an *er* or an *ar?* It's simple enough, if you associate station*er*y with pap*er;* they both have the

Using Instant Memory Power to Master Hard-to-Recall Facts 117

same ending. The same principle (not *pal*) holds true for calend*ar*, linked in your mind with y*ear*.

Another person's gimmick may or may not work for you. But if you create the association yourself, there's a good chance it'll stick like mucilage in your memory.

One secretary, for example, created this simple formula to resolve the farther vs. further controversy. FARther relates to distance, which means, of course, that FURther applies in the figurative sense (he'll go further in his profession). Another girl-Friday seemed constantly perplexed by the affect vs. effect dilemma. But not when she concluded that *a*ffect means to *a*ct upon, while *e*ffect means *e*nd result. There might be a few exceptions, but in most cases, this rule-of-thumb will work quite well.

Learning Words by Association

Because of the dynamic nature of our language, correct pronunciation of rather difficult words poses an occasional problem for most of us. Simply as an isolated example, I used to find myself in a dither over the word *spontaneity*. Do you pronounce it spon-tan-ee-ity or spon-tan-eye-ity? In desperation, I associated it with a roughly synonymous term, *ea*ger. Now if I can just find a place to use the word!

Such manipulation might also help you on occasion in word definition. *Finite,* as a case in point, means measurable. Now for the variations: *finish* means to end; *definitely* means precisely bound; and *infinite* means no bounds at all.

This same principle of association is often used to advantage by students of foreign languages. Foreign words can be learned by rote, of course. But perhaps they will carry more meaning—and be easier to remember—if you can link the foreign word with an English word which means roughly the same thing.

As examples:

English	*Linking Word*	*Foreign Word*
news	novel	nouvelle
wages	salary	salario

English	Linking Word	Foreign Word
road	way	weg
home	domicile	domus
star	stellar	estrella
insanity	demented	demence

"Hard" Numbers Made Easy

Numbers are a pesky lot from your memory's point of view. Perhaps converting them to meaningful words via the key-word alphabet is the best overall solution to the problem. One lady, however, prefers to create little stories to help her remember numbers. Take the telephone number AX 2-2145, for example. She simply remembers the number of times she's been married (twice), then the fact that a 21-year-old girl married a 45-year-old man. This is great, if it works. But she's going to end up with a lot of "stories," which will take some remembering in themselves.

On the other hand, you can frequently run across a true coincidence. Then the number is yours for keeps. Take the telephone number PE 1-2369, for example. Simply visualize the four "corners" of the clock 12-3-6-9, and you have it. Mt. Fujiyama in Japan is a well-known landmark. Not so well-known is the fact that the mountain is 12,365 feet tall. Hard to remember? Not at all, if you can associate it with a calendar: 12 months, 365 days in a year. Now if you can just remember the name of that mountain!

On the other hand, many a school-going youngster found out about clocks by remembering:

> Round and round the
> clock they go,
> Big hand fast and small
> hand slow,
> At what hour do they
> stand,
> For just a moment hand
> in hand?

Developing Your "Miscellaneous Memory"

Your intelligence quotient or educational level doesn't necessarily have a great deal to do with remembering some of life's "basics." For example, there's the schoolteacher who had a hard time remembering whether the light is off or on when the switch is up. See how confusing it gets? Well, she reportedly has little trouble these days. She simply visualizes her friend Colonel *Upizoff,* and she's got it.

A sailor had a devil of a time telling the starboard from the port side of his ship. But not since he walks around on deck with his right hand extended like a star. And sure enough, the right side is the starboard. There was the brilliant woman writer who had to resort to a rather catchy riddle to differentiate east from west. Question: why is the sun like a pancake? Answer: because it rises in der yeast and sets in der vest. And finally, there was the absent-minded professor who couldn't tell a stalactite from a stalagmite. Not so, after he remembered that *tite* suggests something that might cling to the ceiling, while *mite* might be something you see crawling around on the cavern floor. Or perhaps better still, remember that the *c* stands for ceiling, the *g* for ground.

Using an Acrostic for a Crutch

Many a doctor, lawyer, and merchant chief has at one time or another resorted to a good old-fashioned acrostic device to recall some fuzzy bits of information. It works like this. The first letter of a series of unrelated facts is used to spell out a word, such as in the case of the Great Lakes.

H   uron
O   ntario
M   ichigan
E   rie
S   uperior

Or, back in World War II, many ground observers found the WEFT (wings, engine, fuselage, tail) system for identifying aircraft worked amazingly well.

Remember the order of the planets? That's an easy one, if you can recall:

Men	Mercury
Very	Venus
Easily	Earth
Make	Mars
All	Asteroid
Jobs	Jupiter
Serve	Saturn
Useful	Uranus
Needs	Neptune
Promptly	Pluto

Or, if you're in the electronics field, there's a very good chance you recall the seemingly complex color code system by the acrostic:

Bad Boys Ruin Our Young Girls, But Violet Gives Willingly. The colors thus become black, brown, red, orange, yellow, green, blue, violet, gray, and white.

Even medical students can't resist crutches. Or more accurately, since they have volumes of abstract stuff to remember, they rely even more on the acrostic. Many of their devices are downright ingenious, and often a little risqué. Here's one, however, which is mild:

On Old Olympus' Torrid Top,
A Finn and German Picked Some Hops.

Remember this little rhyme and you have virtually recalled all of the cranial nerves: olfactory, optic, oculomotor, trochlear, trigeminal, abducent, facial, auditory, glossopharyngeal, pneumogastric, spinal accessory, and hypoglossal.

Remembering the order of the animal kingdom is a little easier: King Peter Came Over from Germany Seeking a Fortune. This means kingdom, phylum, class, order, family, genus, species, and form, in that order.

Using Instant Memory Power to Master Hard-to-Recall Facts 121

Once entrenched in the memory, an acrostic can be difficult indeed to forget. Realizing this, one speaker entitled his favorite speech, "GROW." "Go Right on Working," that is, and it was widely remembered.

Finally, there is the case of the young preacher, an alumnus of Yale, who was rather proud of his alma mater. So proud, in fact, that he tailored one of his favorite sermons around the YALE acrostic.

In giving his sermon, he would elaborate upon Y (which meant yeoman service to the church); A (asking forgiveness for sins); L (laboring for the Lord); and finally E. As he got to the E, however, one of the young parishioners in the front row was heard to comment: "I'm glad he's not from the Massachusetts Institute of Technology."

You won't always be able to make sense out of such hard-to-remember material. But often the key to success lies in your alertness. In other words, be on the lookout for some meaningful way to remember!

Aghast at the idea of spending the time and effort normally required to memorize hard-to-remember facts, many students will nonetheless go to great lengths to master a catchy mnemonic device.

For example, one youngster was elated to discover that *F*rank*l*in *P*ierce was the *f*ourteenth *P*resident of the United States. He was equally impressed with the fact that Lincoln's first vice-president could be remembered like this: AbraHAM LINcoln. Hamlin, of course, was the man.

Remembering the Presidents

What may take the cake, though, is the way this ingenious college freshman remembered the names of all United States Presidents, in the order in which they served. He simply authored a not-altogether-meaningful story in which he substituted sound-alike words for the names of each President. Once he memorized this fairly short paragraph and learned his word cues, he could write down all the Presidents' names without hesitation.

Here's the story, with the italicized words representing the Presidents—in order:

In *Washington*, *Adams* and *Jeff made money*. *Adams* went to *Jacksonville* to get a *burr haircut* and a *tie* for a *polka*. His *tailor filled more*. *Pierced* by a *cannon*, he *linked* on to *John's grand Hazel* in *garden and field*. As an *author*, he *cleaved* to *hair* and *cleaved* to *magazines*. He *roasted taffy willy-nilly*, but *hardly cooled* his *hoofs*, then *rose* and *truly eyed* his *kin, John's next son*.

The italicized words stand for:

1. Washington	20. Garfield
2. J. Adams	21. Arthur
3. Jefferson	22. G. Cleveland
4. Madison	23. B. Harrison
5. Monroe	24. G. Cleveland
6. J.Q. Adams	25. McKinley
7. Jackson	26. T. Roosevelt
8. Van Buren	27. Taft
9. W.H. Harrison	28. Wilson
10. Tyler	29. Harding
11. Polk	30. Coolidge
12. Taylor	31. Hoover
13. Fillmore	32. F.D. Roosevelt
14. Pierce	33. Truman
15. Buchanan	34. Eisenhower
16. Lincoln	35. Kennedy
17. A. Johnson	36. L. Johnson
18. Grant	37. Nixon
19. Hayes	

Another helpful way to remember a list of disconnected items is to recall them by similar categories, where possible. Take about a minute, for example, to remember this of famous names: Jack Benny, Lana Turner, Richard Nixon, Bob Hope, Sammy Baugh, Ava Gardner, George Burns, Abraham Lincoln, Doak Walker, Raquel Welch, Joe Namath, Bart Starr, Lyndon Johnson, Gina Lollobrigida, and Red Skelton. Now try to jot down these names from memory.

If you were seeking some sort of significant key for remembering this lineup, you might have found that the list is easier to remember if the individuals are grouped together like this: comedians (Hope, Benny, Skelton, and Burns); Presidents (Nixon, Lincoln, and Johnson); football greats (Baugh, Walker, Namath, and Starr); and Hollywood glamor girls (Turner, Gardner, Lollobrigida, and Welch).

In a clutch, try a crutch. It just might work. And it's a "fun" way to add to your instant memory power.

Using Instant Memory Power to Remember Names— Sure-Fire Shortcut to Success   12

"Oh, yes, we've met, what's your name?"

"Jones."

"Oh, I know that. I mean your *first* name."

Such tactics are constantly being used by persons who need to remember names, but just can't. Fortunately, this type of ingenuity, properly channeled, can almost invariably help you to improve your instant memory power in this important area.

Recalling names is one of the most difficult areas of memory for most, and for good reason—most names just don't make sense. If you doubt that a great number of names are downright zany in character, start scanning your telephone directory. Sooner or later, you'll run into such names as Plexico, McLahanan, Masche, Nalweake, Bussiculo, Ouelett, Forte, Persampieri, DiNardo, Dispenziere, Franconcera, Siebuhr, Voje, and a host of others.

You'll find a fair share of Smiths and Jones, too, but unfortunately these names can be just as hard to remember as the jawbreakers. For even these "simple" names rarely make sense, as they relate to a specific individual. For instance, can you think of a Mr. Jones who "looks like" a Mr. Jones?

Psychology of Name-Remembering

Aside from the fact that names don't make sense, most of us don't do too well in this area because we don't use a technique—a uniform approach. In most situations, we fall back on brute memory, which often carries us off on many unproductive tangents.

In addition, there are some subtle psychological and physical forces working against us. Fatigue and alcohol apparently affect memory adversely. Freud says we tend to suppress unpleasant thoughts; for example, "My old flame, I can't even remember her name." A negative attitude, or the power of negative suggestion, can also wreak havoc on the memory. Assume, for example, that you and your friend had seen the same movie recently and knew the names of all characters involved. Suddenly your friend says, "What's the name of the guy who played the lead in that movie we saw?" Before he asked the question, you knew the answer perfectly well. But at the hint that possibly you won't know it, your memory goes blank, at least momentarily.

Giving you a patent "formula" for remembering names is virtually impossible. The techniques we'll suggest must be subject to individual interpretation. Since we all make associations based on our personal experiences, our reaction to a name will be highly "personal" in nature. In addition, a fairly high degree of creative imagination is often required. Thus the more imaginative individual may excel—all other factors being equal—in remembering names.

Accordingly, everyone will probably use the technique just a little differently. This is why it is difficult to lay down hard and fast rules. Instead, consider these suggested techniques as guidelines. They suggest an approach that needs your own personal touch. And bear in mind that the *trained* memory leads to *instant memory power*, especially in the area of names and faces.

The more you use and perfect the technique, the more successfully it will work for you. But don't expect perfection. No person can retain indefinitely all of the names he will be called upon to remember.

Name-remembering not only requires a technique, it calls for using the basic principles of learning and remembering. You must use as many of your memory tools as possible, mainly by taking the sensory approach. You must adopt the proper mental set. And, finally you must recognize that like most learning, name-remembering is accompanied by a certain amount of "pain." You must repeat the name or overlearn it. Barely learned names, like barely learned facts, are subject to short-term residence in your memory.

Following the psychological approach should, in itself, yield some improvement in your name-remembering capability. However, in order to show dramatic improvement, you must go further. You will need to use all your powers of visualization, imagination, and association—in effect, a mnemonic approach—to develop a genuine instant memory power in this important area. The key to success is to train yourself to use these techniques habitually. The techniques must be practiced daily, just as you would practice hitting golf balls or a tennis ball, to excel in those sports.

The principles will be put forth in five "steps." These steps must be performed more or less automatically; which means you must practice until the method becomes second nature to you.

Using Proper Mental Set

The first step is really a state of mind: *show interest and really want to remember the name.*

If you do not have a genuine desire to remember the name, you will rarely do so. As in any learning situation, an appropriate *mental set* is a prerequisite. This involves routinely showing interest, displaying a positive attitude, and genuinely intending to remember.

Further, it helps to establish in your own mind the most positive reason or motive you can think of for remembering the name. Dale Carnegie said it succinctly: "A man's name is to him the sweetest and most important sound in the English language."

Others have echoed the sentiment. Frank Bettger, who wrote, *How I Raised Myself from Failure to Success in Selling Life Insurance* (Prentice-Hall, Inc.), said if he had his career to live over, he would adopt this slogan and hang it over his desk: "Never forget a customer; never let a customer forget you."

Bettger's philosophy was probably prompted by the trouble he had with his own name. Like many names, it is not pronounced like it is spelled. It is pronounced "Betch-yer." This finally prompted the super-salesman and former baseball big-leaguer to create his own gimmick. Upon being introduced, he would say: "My name is Bettger, as in 'Betch-yer life insurance.' " He insisted that the gimmick worked with a majority of business associates and receptionists.

Unfortunately, where Bettger made the task of remembering his name relatively simple, most people confuse the issue by mumbling their name inaudibly during an introduction. To use Bettger's baseball terminology, "You can't hit 'em if you can't see 'em."

With your motive firmly set, your interest level high, and your intentions honorable and positive, you have evolved the right frame of mind or attitude for remembering the name.

Selecting an Outstanding Feature

Step two is: *"Identify" the person by selecting what appears to you to be an outstanding physical characteristic.* The idea is to link the person's name and his physical makeup in such a way that these two elements are remembered together. This is a realistic approach, for, in remembering a name, you must also remember what the person looks like. Almost everyone has good visual memory. We can recall, perhaps in some detail, the faces of many whom we knew many years ago—even from childhood. But the name, alas, is gone forever from conscious memory.

The recommended procedure is to select some feature of the person which is outstanding—or which appears prominent to you—and use this as a focal point for identification. For example, if a man has black, wavy hair, make a mental note of this fact. This is the feature you will visually recognize when trying to remember his name later. If the feature appears to be a high forehead, or perhaps a distinctively shaped neck, select these. Or you might be impressed by his overall stature—short or tall, slender or stout.

Being able to spot an identifiable feature quickly is a talent that usually has to be developed. Law-enforcement agencies claim the average citizen is woefully inept at identifying people. There is room for improvement, even in the best of us. Caricature artists are "naturals" at selecting prominent features and exaggerating these features in a sketch. Perhaps, with practice, some of the know-how will rub off on you. "Once you select the outstanding feature, there is a tendency for this recollection to help you visualize the other features, bringing the entire face into perspective," one well-known commercial artist says.

There is still another virtue in selecting a feature; this step routinely gives you a point of departure. Linking the person and his name together is a crucial step and a logical point from which to start a name-remembering attempt.

Again, one of the reasons most of us have trouble remembering names is that we fail to use, routinely, a standard method in the recall process. We start to remember the name, and our thoughts scatter in all directions. We try to recall where we met the person, what he was wearing, what he said, and how he looked. All sorts of things run through our mind. All these things can be important, as mentioned in the previous reference to "redintegration." However, in using this type approach, we are scattershooting. The advantage of going back to the prominent feature is that it gives you a *standard* point of departure. It can, on occasion, also serve as the focal point around which you might want to make an interesting visual association.

Starting at the top, the hair might be particularly noticeable for a number of reasons: too much or too little; receding hairline;

striking color; burr haircut; or some of the more faddish styles. The forehead itself is sometimes characteristically low or high, or the lines in the forehead may serve as a feature tag.

Eyebrows and eyes can be used on occasion. They may be quite pronounced, or the opposite, very thin. Or they may slant in an unusual way. Eyes are sometimes characterized as "wide open," "narrow," or "slanting."

The nose potentially has more "shapes" than any other feature. It might be characteristically small or large, pug, convex, pointed, long, or short.

Lips can sometimes be noticeably full, short, or wide. The chin, on the other hand, has a wide range of shapes, all the way from jutting to receding, round, square, cleft, and a good many configurations in between.

A bull-like neck would likely be noticed, as would a long, slender neck. The ears probably are noticed only in rare cases.

On the other hand, the outstanding feature might be the person's overall size. You might note, significantly, that the person is rather short, or the opposite, quite tall. He may appear to be husky or slender. Anything, in short, which is noticeable at the outset to you might be the feature tag you will use in your identification of the person.

Sometimes, the feature you select will be determined to a large extent by the name itself. It may literally "tie in" with the name. For example: Phillips and "full lips."

At Scotland Yard, inspectors are trained to never observe a face without noticing some outstanding feature. Officials feel that you become highly observant mainly from habit.

The best way to identify a person would be to take his photograph, then refer to it later on. This is impractical, so the next best thing is to furnish your own "photograph" from your mind's eye. In other words, make such a vivid impression that the outstanding feature will serve to bring the entire face back into focus.

A good way to test your powers of observation is to try to sketch the face of the person you recently met. Or, if you're not artistically inclined, write down from memory a description of that person. If the face is a blur, or if you failed to come up with an outstanding feature, you undoubtedly failed to observe well during the introduction. And chances are you'll have a hard time remembering his name. The final step is to compare your drawing or your written description with the real person to see how accurately you performed.

Getting the Name Right

Now that you've gotten yourself mentally set to remember the name and have identified the person by selecting what appears to you to be an outstanding feature, you're ready for step three: *get the name right and repeat it.*

Undoubtedly, one of the main reasons we don't remember a great number of names is that we don't hear the name correctly in the first place. Being "polite," most of us are reluctant to ask a person to repeat the name, or spell it—or even better, both. Clearly, you cannot remember the name if you fail to "catch it" accurately in the first place. It is mandatory that you not only pin the name down correctly, but also repeat it as many times as possible. Speak the name aloud if possible; in any case, say it silently. It helps still further to write it down, giving you a visual impression.

The sensory approach, you will recall, is considered effective, since it brings into play your primary "learning channels"—your eyes and ears. Gentleman Jim Farley apparently used the sensory approach to great advantage in his name-remembering exploits.

First, Farley would make certain he heard the name correctly. This no doubt involved asking a question such as: "What was that name again; I didn't catch it?" Or, "That's an unusual name, the first time I've heard it I believe." Or, "How many of you are there in the phone book?" Most people, Farley contends, are not offended when you belabor the point of remembering their name. Quite the opposite, they're flattered at the attention.

This poses a problem of sorts for some. How do you unobtrusively mention the name aloud several times? A politician like

Farley probably finds the technique relatively simple. For example, he might ask a question such as: "Mr. Wackerbarth. That's an interesting name. Where did it originate?" Or, "That's interesting Mr. Wackerbarth." And finally, "Nice to have met you Mr. Wackerbarth." Admittedly, this approach won't work on Mr. Jones. You may have to give him the "silent" treatment.

This routine helps entrench a name in your memory. And it helps in making a strong auditory impression. To carry out the multiple-sensory approach, Farley, when time permitted, would later write the name down. This enabled him to see the name and make a stronger visual connection. While all this was going on, Farley was busy making meaningful associations.

Repeating the name—the *right* name—is quite important. So important, in fact, that one psychologist completed experiments which showed that this step alone will help you to remember the name 34% better.

Having tackled your name-remembering assignment in the proper frame of mind, you're now ready for some mental acrobatics. The key to an instant memory power for names is in making meaningful associations. This gives the name *meaning;* it is an indispensable step if you wish to retain the name for a long period of time.

An association can be either mental or visual. Hopefully, you will frequently be able to make both types of association, since the multiple-association technique is more effective. "Multiple associations," Farley said, "give you more hooks on which you can hang things." The more associations you make with any one object, the more likely you are to recall it later. For example, you meet a Mr. Sullen and think of him as being of a *sullen* nature; this is a mental association. If, in addition, you can visualize a sullen person with mouth turned down, you have made a visual association. Don't forget, a strong mental picture can be quite helpful in reminding you of a specific object or *name.*

The idea is to make a multiple association wherever possible, using both mental and visual associations. One of the best ways to do this is literally to "assault" the name when you hear it. Be ready to associate it with as many things as you can possibly think of that make sense to you. The rather unusual name of Perrett, for example, might normally give your memory a fit. Here's how you might kick the name around in your mind.

First, do you know someone else by the same name? If this fails, your only immediate response might be to substitute a sound-alike word (based on the law of similarity of sound). In this case, how about *parrot?* Parrot sounds like Perrett and will likely be an effective reminder. To help further, visualize a parrot on the person's outstanding physical feature. Or, maybe the word sounds more like *pirouette.* In this case, visualize a ballerina whirling away on the same feature.

The degree of success you will enjoy will depend, in large measure, on how adept you become at quickly giving the name meaning. You should obviously become more effective as you continue to practice. The main idea is to make it a habit to *look for meaning,* and this cannot be done passively. Avoid the tendency to think, "Gosh, I just can't make any sense out of this name at all." You have to work at it.

Many of the associations you will make will be artificial, and to a large extent, tentative in nature. This is precisely why you should make as many meaningful associations as possible. If you forget one, perhaps you'll remember another.

How to Remember First Names

Remembering last names is probably more important in the business world, where you can introduce or recall someone as *Mr.* Jones or *Mrs.* Jones, at least for starters. But frequently, a first-name basis is more desirable.

Quite often, after you've learned the last name, the first name will "fall into place." But you can't depend on this happening, so it's best, where possible, to pay considerable attention to the first name, or in some instances, a nickname.

One of the most logical, and certainly the easiest route to follow, is to associate the person's first name with someone you know who has the same first name. If you were to meet Adolph Pareman, you could associate him with other Adolphs of your acquaintance, making sure that you note similar or opposite features or personality traits. Try to visualize them together. If you can't think of a personal acquaintance named Adolph, pick a well-known personality like Hitler. Here's a guy you'd like to forget, but can't because of the notoriety he achieved. Maybe this will lead to an even more interesting and vivid mental picture!

You can sometimes use an acrostic-like device to help you remember the first name, or, in some cases the entire name. Let's assume that Adolph Pareman had been introduced as A.F. Pareman. Using *pear* as a symbol for the last name, form two meaningful words with the same initials, such as: *A*ffable, *F*riendly *pear*. The words you would use would no doubt be conditioned largely by the impression the person made on you. In this case, we're assuming he was quite friendly; thus, "affable" and "friendly" fit.

Or, assuming again that you knew him only as Adolph Pareman, you might use the key-word alphabet approach (remember, vowels don't count). In this case, the acrostic for *A*dolph *P*areman could be *AP*e, if he's hairy; or *A*l*P* if he's tall; and so forth.

If the word you select is appropriate, the acrostic can be just as effective a reminder as HOMES was for the Great Lakes. Remember?

There's still another way to help tie that first name down, but it requires an extraordinary knowledge of first-name derivations. Most popular names are derived from Latin, Hebrew, or Teutonic words that had a different meaning many years ago. Benedict used to mean "blessed," for example, while Leroy stood for "royal."

Knowing the original meaning of some of the more popular names can sometimes help you make a meaningful association with the first name. Had you, for example, known the origin of Adolph, you might have been able to come up with an effective association based on this knowledge. Adolph stands for "noble hero." It might have fit nicely if Adolph had been a football star or a war hero. In any case, this knowledge would no doubt have forced you to think along these lines.

Below is a partial list of some of the more popular names and what they stand for:

Women

Abigail, my father is joy
Agatha, good or kind
Agnes, chaste or pure
Alice or Alicia, truth
Alma, cherishing
Amanda, worthy to be loved
Amy, beloved
Ann, Anna, grace
Avia, bird
Barbara, strange
Beatrice, she that makes happy
Belle, beautiful
Beulah, married
Bridget, august
Carmen, song
Caroline, feminine of Charles
Celeste, heavenly
Clara, bright or illustrious
Constance, firmness
Daphne, laurel
Deborah, a bee
Diana, goddess
Dinah, judged
Dolores, sorrows
Edna, rejuvenation
Elizabeth, consecrated to God
Ethel, noble
Eunice, happy victory
Eve, living

Women

Evelyn, youth
Felicia, happiness
Gertrude, spear maiden
Gloria, glory
Grace, favor
Hilda, battle maid
Irene, peace
Iris, rainbow
Judith, praised
Laura, laurel
Leila, dark as night
Letitia, happiness
Lillian, lily
Lydia, native of Lydia
Martha, lady or mistress
Matilda, mighty battle maid or heroine
Melissa, bee
Minnie, love (often nickname for Mary)
Naomi, my sweetness
Olive, an olive
Penelope, a weaver
Phoebe, shining
Phyllis, a green bough
Prudence, discretion
Rachel, ewe
Rosalind, pretty rose
Salome, peace
Sara, a princess
Sophia, wisdom
Stella, a star
Susan, lily
Ursula, she-bear
Victoria, victory

Men

Abel, vanity
Abner, my father is near
Abraham, uncertain meaning
Adolph, noble wolf or noble hero
Albert, illustrious through nobility
Alexander, defender of men
Alfred, good counselor
Alvin, noble
Amos, borne
Andrew, strong or manly
Arnold, strong as an eagle
Aubrey, ruler
Benedict, blessed
Benjamin, son of right hand
Bernard, bold as a bear
Cecil, dim-sighted
Charles, strong or manly
Christopher, bearing Christ
Dan, a judge
David, beloved
Dexter, on right hand, fortunate
Donald, world ruler
Duncan, brown warrior
Earl, noble
Edgar, protector of property
Edmund, defender of property
Edward, guardian of property
Edwin, gainer of property
Elmer, noble and famous
Eugene, well-born
Felix, happy or prosperous
Francis, free
Franklin, a freeman

Men

Gabriel, man of God
George, a husbandman
Gerald, spear-wielder
Gilbert, bright wish
Godfrey, peace of God
Gregory, vigilant
Guy, a leader
Harold, army leader
Henry, ruler of private property
Herbert, glory of the army
Herman, a warrior
Hilary, cheerful or merry
Hiram, most noble
Hugh, mind
Ira, watchful
Isaac, laughter
Jack, familiar form of John
Jacob, a supplanter
John, God is gracious
Joseph, he shall add
Leo, lion
Leonard, brave as a lion
Leroy, royal
Levi, joining
Lionel, young lion
Louis, famous warrior
Lucius, light
Luther, illustrious warrior
Martin, war-like
Matthew, gift of Jehovah
Maurice, dark-colored
Michael, who is like God?
Nathan, gift

Men

Nathaniel, gift of God
Neal or Neil, courageous
Nicholas, victorious army
Norman, a Northman
Patrick, a patrician
Paul, little
Peter (Pierre), a rock
Philip, love of horses
Quentin, the fifth
Raymond, wise protection
Reginald, strong ruler
Reuben, behold a son
Richard, strong like a ruler, powerful
Robert, bright in fame
Roderick, rich in fame
Roger, famous with the spear
Roy, king
Rufus, red-haired
Seth, appointed
Silvester, rustic
Solomon, peaceable
Stephen, crown
Theodore, gift of God
Thomas, a twin
Timothy, honoring God
Ulysses, a hater
Victor, conqueror
Vincent, conquering
Walter, ruling the host
Wilfred, desire for peace
William, resolute helmet
Winfred, win peace

A fuller list of names is available in many dictionaries. You can't learn them all at once. But if you can learn a few names at a time, this knowledge can serve as a useful—and often entertaining—way to remember a first name.

By and large, however, you'll want to concentrate on remembering that all-important last name, and following are some of the main areas in which you can look for an association. In actual practice, you'll no doubt find yourself using various combinations of these steps, based on your own experience and ability to imagine.

Tying in with an Outstanding Feature

Tie in the name with a physical characteristic. Again, the physical feature you choose may sometimes be conditioned by the name itself. In other words, the name and the feature tag simply "go together" as far as you're concerned. For example, I once met a very dignified-looking man at a luncheon. To me, his most noticeable feature was rather prominent eyebrows. By coincidence (but remember, I was looking for it) his name turned out to be Mr. Bush. An exception? Yes, but the fact remains that such associations are there often enough if you are mentally set for them.

You might run into a Mr. Sharp, who happens to have a rather sharp-pointed nose (now that you think of it). You might in the same breath make note of the fact that he is mentally sharp. Then there's Mr. Bay. You guessed it; he's got a pretty good bay window.

How about Mr. Beard? Upon hearing the name, assuming you are in an associative frame of mind, you notice that he has a "heavy beard." There is a slight shadow, even though he appears to have just shaven. Then there's Mr. Coombs. Since a comb reminds you of hair, it's easy enough to note that he has thick, healthy hair—an outstanding physical feature you can easily remember.

One of the techniques we will discuss shortly involves substituting a similar-sounding word. This technique is based on the

Using Instant Memory Power to Remember Names—Shortcut to Success 141

law of similarity. With slight variations, it can be combined with the technique of associating with an outstanding physical feature.

You are introduced, for example, to Mr. O'Hara, who happens to have a full head of blonde hair. This is your physical tag. The words "O'Hara" and "hair" have the same rhyme; thus, one word could easily remind you of the other. Or, perhaps he is bald, which means "no O'Hara" at all. A Mr. Langley is next in line of introduction, and you notice that he is tall and slender, "lanky" that is. Since you have made a mental note of the fact, "Langley" and "lanky" become quite similar in sound, and hopefully, you'll remember the two together. Names such as Green, Gray, Black, White, Brown, and others also lend themselves frequently to the person's coloring or some other feature. These names fall into another category which we'll discuss shortly.

The importance of learning to associate the person's name with some outstanding physical characteristic can't be overstressed. At times, this may be the only immediate area in which you can make a meaningful association. At any rate, it'll be an excellent starting point for making a multiple-association with the name.

The possibilities for tying a person's name to his physical feature, using visualization, are almost infinite. It's impossible to lay down rigid rules, because the associations you make must be based on *your* experience and background and the manner in which *you* size up the person and the situation. However, here are some samples to give you an indication of the general approach to be used.

Let's assume that you meet a person who has red hair; this is almost certain to be your physical feature tag. His name is Felix Turner. You'll undoubtedly think of some other areas of association for this name, but for now let's confine it to the physical feature. Turner doesn't seem to tie in logically with red hair. But perhaps "burner" does, so how about picturing a *burner* on Turner, visualizing the burner on that red hair, of course. For the full name, try the acrostic FaT, which may fit in either a similar or opposite manner. You probably aren't aware of it, but the name Felix stands for "happy or prosperous." Maybe this would fit, too.

Very convenient, you say, that the man with red hair is named Felix Turner. All right, we'll change the picture: The redhead is a woman, Hilda Gardner. The red hair is still the focal point of our association, so let's say, for memory's sake, that you "dig" the red hair, and you visualize a *gardner* doing his spade work in Miss Gardner's red hair. As you can imagine, such an act would probably infuriate this lovely redhead. Applying the acrostic to the name, you can get HaG, or a more pleasant idea, HuG. Hilda, incidentally, stands for "battle maid," for whatever that might be worth.

The same principle can be applied to other physical features: eyes, ears, forehead, nose, and general head shape.

Let's take a person with a Durante-type nose, for example, and give him several different names to see how the idea works. For starters, let's try the name *Patterson* (how about visualizing the ex-heavyweight champ Floyd Patterson battering away at your new friend's nose); suppose the name is *Graham* (picture yourself sweeping up Graham crackers from his big proboscis, or envision a *gray ham* about the same size as his nose); for the name *Grove* (visualize perhaps an orange *grove* or an orange being thrown at his nose; for *Adams* (picture Adam, with or without Eve, or perhaps an *atomic* explosion); for *Underwood* (picture the nose buried under a pile of wood, or place a big typewriter on it). You can make this type association process work on almost any name, although some names will require considerable creative effort.

If you really work on it, you can in many cases work out an effective association using the main physical characteristic, using either the first or last name—or perhaps both.

Generally, it's not wise to use a person's dress as a focal point for an association; he probably won't be wearing the same clothes the next time you see him. But don't rule out the possibility of using eyeglasses, which are frequently regarded as "trademarks" for some people.

How often, for example, have you heard a person describe someone by saying something like this: "Oh, you know, he's sort of tall and slender and wears horn-rimmed glasses." I fit that description fairly closely and wear horn-rimmed glasses most of the time. This being the case, I used to give people a chance to associate me with Robert Q. Lewis, erstwhile television performer. Admittedly, that's a tailor-made association. The association would be more difficult if the name were, say, Sullivan or Wagner. But there's always a way. In these cases, you might form a vivid mental picture by visualizing John L. Sullivan, and asking Mr. Sullivan to "take off those glasses," or you might use the glasses as a platform for a Wagnerian opera. Other types of glasses which might serve as a "trademark" include those that are rimless, metal-rimmed, heavily tinted, or extremely modern.

Putting these principles to work, let's meet a few people at a small social gathering. From left to right, there's:

SAM CARTER (short, stout build, wide mouth): How about popping some CARTER's pills into Sam's mouth; or visualize yourself pushing a CART across his mouth; or think of him as Nick CARTER, private eye. Surely you can think of another SAM (even if it's your uncle). An interesting acrostic might be SaC, or using the mouth as your feature tag, SuCK.

MARTHA SMOTHERS (medium height, attractive, highly arched eyebrows): Picture the SMOTHERS Brothers performing on the arched eyebrows; or maybe you want to SMOTHER her with kisses—on the eyebrows, that is. MARTHA, interestingly enough, stands for "lady or mistress."

HAROLD HUMPHREY (large, distinguished appearance, white hair): Using the hair as a platform, visualize Hubert HUMPHREY orating with gusto; also note the similarity in initials, HH. In desperation, you might picture him getting over the HUMP (his white hair) *free*.

RUFUS MILTON (slight build, long black hair and sideburns, sunken cheeks): The esthetic appearance reminds you of MILTON, the poet, whom you can place in a mental picture, using either the long hair or the sideburns, or both. Does the acrostic RuM help?

HENRY ROSS (tall, slender, long nose, wears rimless glasses):

ROSS sounds like ROSE, so you might visualize a big red rose on HENRY's nose; another tack might be to picture ex-boxer, Barney ROSS, punching on that delicate proboscis. Can you associate him with another HENRY? Or, how about the old standby, "Quick, HENRY, the Flit."

SOPHIA VALENTINO (short, stout build, mole on left cheek): Nothing "Hollywood" about Sophia, except, of course, her name. So, using the rule of opposites, visualize SOPHIA Loren on her mole, maybe doing a tango with the heartthrob of the silent movies, Rudolph VALENTINO. The acrostic is SaVe, for whatever that's worth. And SOPHIA means wisdom.

Obviously, the more you practice, the more adept you become at making meaningful associations with the outstanding feature.

Meeting a large group of people is an extremely difficult assignment. You simply apply the principles we've discussed, only more vigorously. At least try to slow down the introductions to give you more time to assimilate the names. Many find it helpful to "learn" the names beforehand so that they can form tentative associations. Anything, in short, which will help you remember the names should be taken into account.

Finding Other Areas of Association

Use a Business or Hobby. A few years ago, a gentleman by the unlikely name of Bob Shotwell "fired" the first *Atlas* missile. Had you been mentally set to capitalize on such a rare coincidence, you would have probably noted that Bob did fire the missile quite well. To stretch a point, it was "shot well."

The fact that a name "ties into" the person's profession or avocation is a happy one. For some obscure reason, we rarely forget what line of work a person is in. So if the name can be tied in logically with his work, the association becomes a "natural" one.

For example, Mr. Stone is a contractor, while Mr. Cook is a chef. Mr. Justice is a crime reporter; Mrs. Saylers is a secretary for the Maritime Commission; and Mr. Pigg and Mr. Landrum are farm writers.

Using this technique with the "sound alike" principle, we find that Mr. Keyhoe is an investigator of unidentified flying objects and other psychic phenomena. It is difficult—no, virtually impossible—to hear the name Keyhoe without instantly thinking of the word "keyhole." Phonetically, they are so similar that they are almost impossible to tell apart. His unusual profession, then, jibes with his name.

Mr. Foster is an instructor of a speed-reading course. In this case, a sound-alike substitute can be significant; momentarily, he can become Mr. *Faster,* for obvious reasons. What are the chances of your calling him by the substitute word rather than the real name? Rather remote. Logic dictates that the name simply can't be *Faster*—rather, Foster.

Use Birthplace or Address. Name-remembering is such an arduous task that you must use every bit of help you can get. You'll be able to use the birthplace or address only rarely. But these items can offer an effective memory peg. For example, there's: Mr. Evans from Evansville, Indiana; Mr. Adams, who lives on Adams Street; Mr. Bell from Liberty Street; Mr. Haile on Rufe Snow Drive; Mrs. Hunt on Slaughter Street; and Mr. Price on Fortune Road.

Associate the Name with Someone (or Something) You Know. Perhaps the first and most important step to take in remembering names is to link the name with something you're familiar with. If you meet Mr. Jones or Mr. Smith, for example, you can certainly think of several of your friends who have the same name. Make a mental connection between your new friend and the old one; then visualize them together. Perhaps you noted similar—or opposite—traits. You have thus linked the old with the new, and quite likely you have made an effective association. This particular technique gains added importance as you proceed in this risky business of name-remembering. Unusual names like Etier, Egly, and Strump will likely give you some trouble the first time around. But when you come across the name again, assuming you're in the proper mental set, you probably will find it difficult *not* to think of your old "friend" with the same name.

The name you're trying to remember need not be linked to a

person as such. It can be tied into an institution or thing you happen to be familiar with. This still gives you the advantage of tying the old and the new together. And most of us "know" of hundreds of such things through advertising and by simply keeping abreast of the new.

It's difficult, for example, *not* to hear the name Webster without almost instantly associating it with the dictionary. To be sure, there are a number of other associations which can be made with this name, but this is undoubtedly the consensus reaction to the word. This gives you an instant mental connection between your new acquaintance and the known factor—*Webster's Dictionary*. For good measure, try visualization to anchor the name down more firmly. Assume, in this case, that the outstanding feature happens to be Mr. Webster's crew-cut hair. It can easily support, visually speaking, a full-size dictionary.

Now you meet Mrs. Dial, and you select as a feature tag her dark, full eyes. The name Dial should instantly bring to mind a number of familiar persons and things. A football enthusiast might visualize Buddy Dial, the ex-pro football star; he's catching a touchdown pass right there in those limpid eyes. A soap by the same name comes to mind (note that she's clean-cut). Visually, this fact makes an interesting mental picture possible; Mrs. Dial showering with her Dial soap. There's also the verb dial. Visualize a telephone and have Mrs. Dial chatting away. Maybe you can even hear the "dial" tone.

Suppose you meet a Mr. DiMaggio. You probably don't have to be a baseball buff to visualize Joltin' Joe, the famed Yankee Clipper. In fact, it's almost impossible *not* to make this association. Or, you might think of his former wife, Marilyn Monroe. Any one of these ideas lends itself to an interesting mental picture.

Now you're introduced to a Mrs. Royal, whom you identify by her raven black hair. If she is, by coincidence, a secretary, you can readily associate her with a well-known typewriter; and you can make an interesting visual picture while you're at it. There's also a pudding by the same name, if you elect to visualize her in domestic surroundings. The word royal also connotes a regal character which you might attribute to the woman.

Using Instant Memory Power to Remember Names—Shortcut to Success 147

The same principle can be used in connection with a number of names. Either you know a person by the same name, or you are familiar with the product or institution the name brings to mind. To this extent, it is "familiar." So names like Heinz, Ford, Hoover, Firestone, Gaines, Kellogg—and countless others—have considerable significance for most people.

The Name Connects with a Catchy Jingle or Slogan. Advertisers feel, with some justification, that the public can remember a catchy slogan after hearing it only once or twice. Why? Probably, at least in part, because of the law of similarity of sound. A pun may be the lowest form of humor, but it is also one of the easiest things to remember.

For example, there was a lawyer named Mr. Hull. His motto: "Tell the truth, the *hull* truth, and nothing but the truth." With apologies (unless, of course, the idea helps you to remember the name), here are a few more real-life examples:

Mr. Dewey (the salesman) is full of hooey. Mr. Rand (a musician) plays in the band. Mr. Flynn is naturally "in like Flynn." Mr. Givens is noted for his ability to "Given' take," in business transactions that is. Of Mr. Hurst we recall, "It only Hurst for a little while." And Mr. Stanley is naturally linked with "Stanley and Livingston."

This approach usually requires considerable creative imagination, such as one student used in remembering Mrs. Krietz, a former airline stewardess. He suggested that she "go fly a Krietz."

Following this same pattern, it often helps to use a well-known nickname as a memory-jogger. For example, if you meet a Mr. Rhoades, you can, privately at least, take the liberty of calling him by his nickname, "Dusty." He's undoubtedly been called that before. At any rate, this is hopefully only one of several connections you will make with the name in the process of creating a multiple association.

Use the Meaning the Name Has in Itself. Lane, Meek, Nichols, Taylor, Robbins, Stout, Spikes, Roach, Pope, Witt, Hunter, Nabers, Day, Brown, White, Cable. These and countless other names—or *words*—have meaning in themselves. The word almost automatically forms the basis for an effective association. Recall the *word* and you have remembered the name. Spelling, as such, makes little difference in these cases; for example, the name Nichols is pronounced the same as *nickels* (5 cent pieces).

Now, visualization becomes important. Let's assume, as an example, that you are actually meeting this Mr. Nichols. You notice his ears as an outstanding feature; then fill the ears, visually that is, with a lot of nickels. Or, perhaps better still, have someone hitting the jackpot, and nickels will pour forth in a steady stream from his ears.

Next up, Mr. White. His name being "meaningful," you will probably note that there is a touch of white in his hair. Now meet Mr. Stout, or Mr. Strong. In these cases, you will no doubt make a mental note of their physical makeup: short, tall, slender, stout. Then make an association, based on either the law of similarity or the law of opposites. For example, isn't it a coincidence that Mr. Stout is so frail?

Then there's Mr. Steel. Under the circumstances, you'll probably note his "steely" eyes. Perhaps you'll also note that he has muscles like steel, or that he stands straight, like a steel beam. There's also the possibility that the ladies might look upon him as a man who might *steal* their heart away. This name (or word), like many others in this category, lends itself to vivid mental pictures.

The main idea is to give added significance to a name or word that already has meaning to you. You simply use the word in the literal sense. As a *word*, it has meaning; as a name, it usually does not. Your objective, remember, is to give the name *meaning*.

Substitute a Word with Similar Sound. The principle here is the same as the one used in the preceding step. You try to take a meaningless word and give it meaning.

Let's say you are introduced to a Mr. Leon, a name which to you has virtually no significance. You can think of no one with the same name, and the name, at least for the moment, doesn't lend itself to a jingle. In such cases, the only "logical" step is to

Using Instant Memory Power to Remember Names—Shortcut to Success 149

substitute a similar-sounding word, trusting that the law of similarity will work for you. *Lion* is the substitute word in this case, and it is something that you can readily visualize. Let's assume that the gentleman has a receding hairline. Now you simply insert a picture of your mighty *lion* prowling around in the vicinity, tearing out a little hair here and there. The contrast of the shaggy *lion* and the hairless Mr. Leon should afford an interesting paradox.

How about Mr. Adyman? The name is, for all practical purposes, meaningless. But you'll have to admit it sounds a great deal like "ad man." Since you have selected, say, his cleft chin as an outstanding feature tag, simply visualize him as an ad man there, working away on a clever ad campaign.

By the same token, a name like Freidham sounds like freedom; Chollar like collar; Lowke like luck; Philpot like full pot; Conitt like conduit or can-do-it.

There is, of course, some danger of calling the person by the sound-alike word rather than the name itself, but the chances of your doing so are remote. In most cases, common sense will help you to "eliminate" the sound-alike word in recalling the name. For example, in the above illustration, have you ever known of a person named Lion or Ad Man? Not likely.

Break the Name Down into Meaningful Syllables. Some names virtually defy "instant remembering." These are usually the long, hard-to-pronounce names. But, a longer name like Swearingen might break down into the phrase "swear in gin," which gives you meaningful words to work with and at the same time lends itself to vivid mental imagery. Or, in remembering a name like Bowcowski, you might break it down into a picture of the man getting ready to *bow* to a *cow* on *skis*. A ridiculous image, true. But it does create a semblance of logic, where none existed before.

The final step is to review. Try visualizing the person. Recall the name. Write it down if you are able to do so. Ebbinghaus, you'll recall, found that something barely learned is barely retained. Overlearning, on the other hand, tends to help you remember more efficiently. Thus if a name is not reviewed, it stands a good chance of being lost to conscious memory. Names are unquestionably more susceptible to the forgetting curve than more meaningful facts and ideas. Review is an extremely important step to take if you plan to remember the name "permanently."

Mastering the technique of remembering names is a great deal like learning to use shorthand effectively. The technique must be practiced until it can be used automatically and with imagination. As in the learning phase of any technique, you will probably be painfully aware at the outset of the various "steps" involved. But after you practice over a period of time—taking success with failure—you will be able to perform the routine smoothly and effectively.

Testing Yourself on Names

As a starter, let's practice on several new acquaintances. In each case, select an outstanding feature which will help you identify the person. Then try to make an association that is meaningful to you. Some of the associations mentioned will work for you; others will not. In every case, you will want to inject a few personal associations of your own. And don't forget to repeat the name. (See page 152.)

PHOTO SERIES FOLLOWS ⟶

Mr. BOOTH

Meet Mr. BOOTH. "BOOTH tells the truth." At least he should; he's a lawyer. You surely know someone with the same name, even if it's John Wilkes BOOTH. To help your "mental" memory, visualize him in a telephone BOOTH, calling a client. Now you know the truth about Mr. BOOTH.

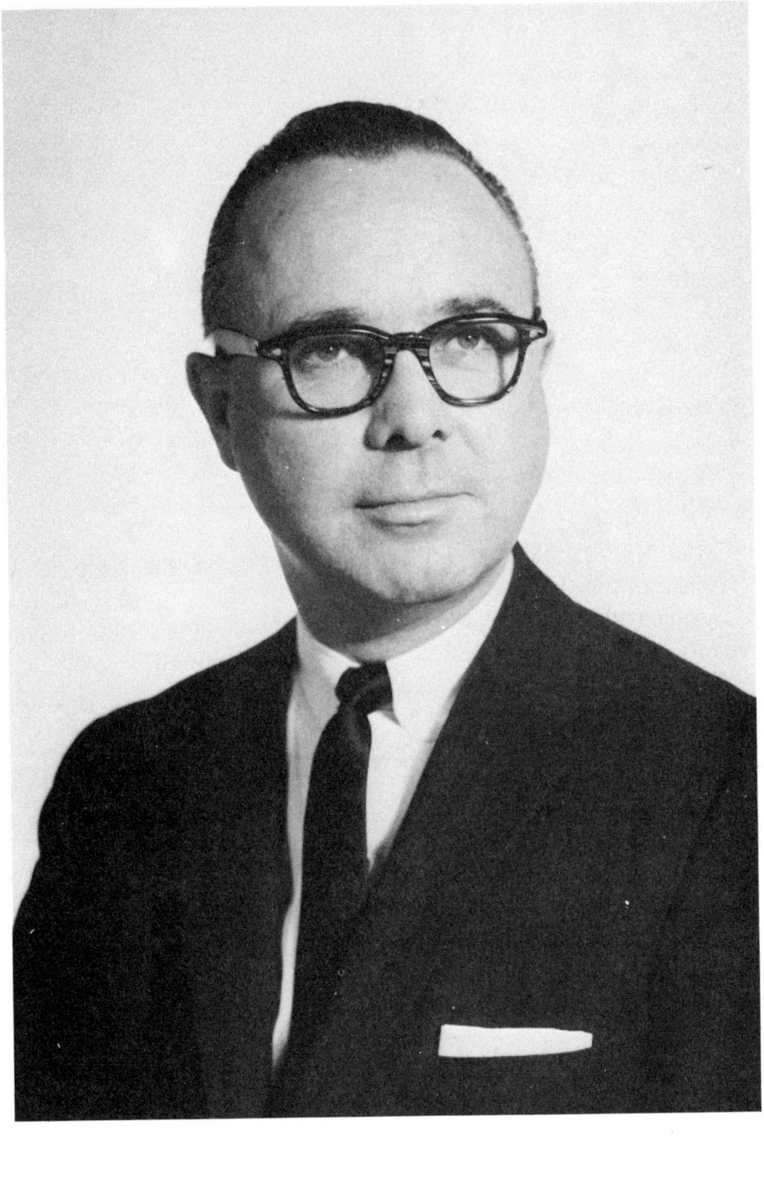

Mrs. TILLEY

Meet Mrs. TILLEY. It rhymes with silly, but nothing could be further from the truth. Mrs. TILLEY is anything but silly; she's a genuine Phi Beta Kappa with bathing-beauty proportions. The former Miss Dallas, no less. So instead of silly, how about "dilly." Mrs. TILLEY is a dilly. Agreed?

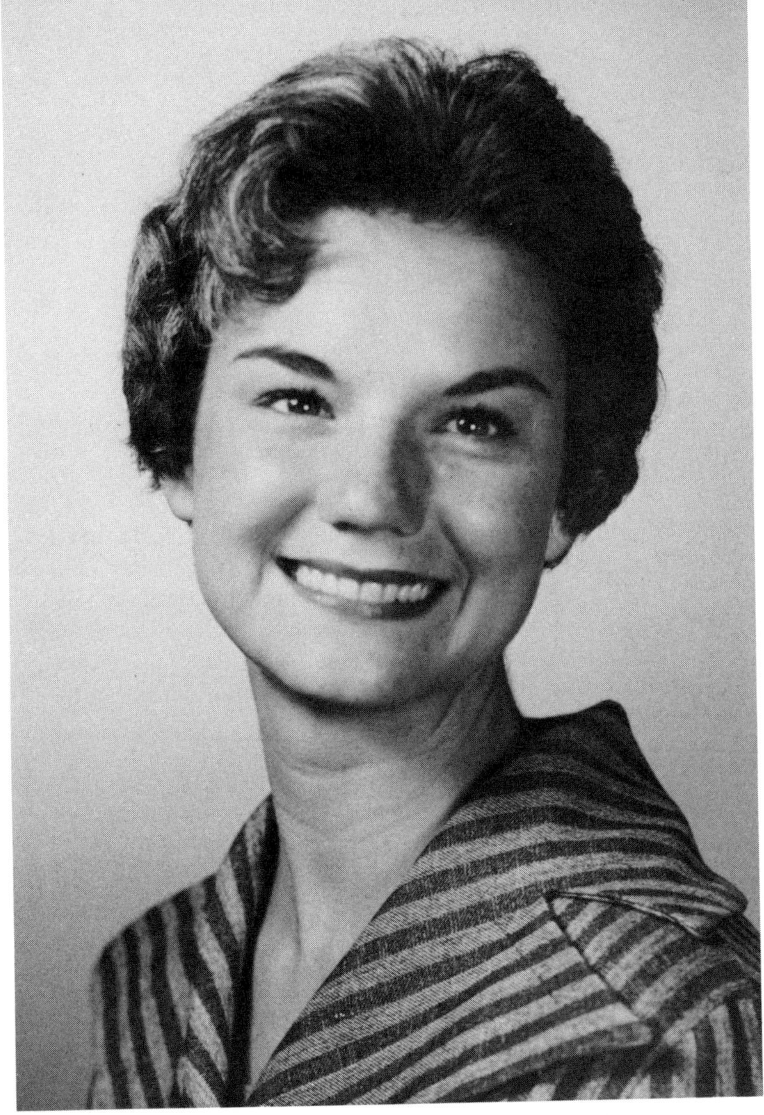

Mr. DeMANCHE

Meet Mr. DeMANCHE. An illustrator, Mr. DeMANCHE has a name that sounds like Da Vinci, the artist. To remember Mr. DeMANCHE, visualize Da Vinci painting a portrait on Mr. DeMANCHE's outstanding feature (perhaps that cleft chin). On the other hand, baseball enthusiasts might like to associate DeMANCHE with DiMAGGIO (same rhythm). But remember, it's Mr. DeMANCHE.

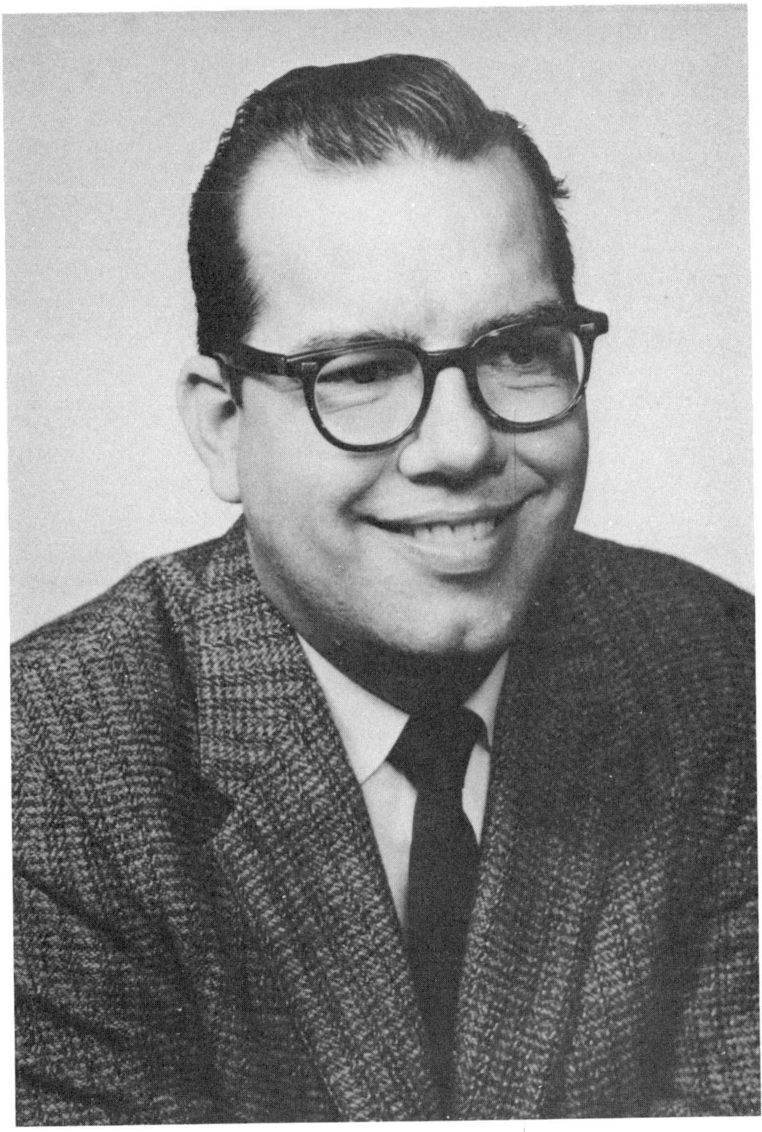

Mr. ELDER

Meet Mr. ELDER. Note that fine crew haircut, which makes this retired Air Force colonel appear quite young. However, that dignified looking patch of gray above his temple makes him look a little ELDER. For good measure, you might want to visualize Mr. ELDER, the church ELDER, conducting services there. Remember youthful-looking Mr. ELDER.

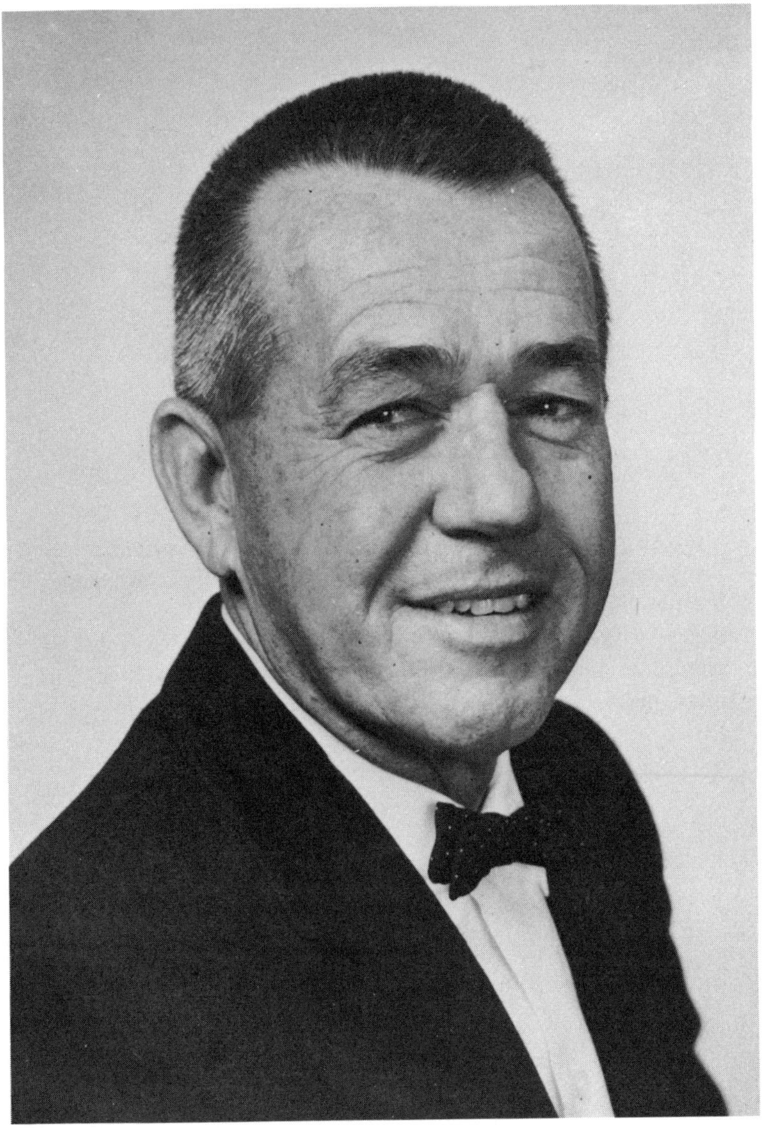

Mr. NUTT

Meet Mr. NUTT. As you can imagine, Mr. NUTT is the butt of many bad puns (the better to remember him by). Nicknames include "Wall," "Cashew" and "Pea," to name a few. You can make up your own and at the same time create a vivid mental picture to remember him by. Keeping the law of opposites in mind, make a mental memo: Mr. NUTT is a PhD.

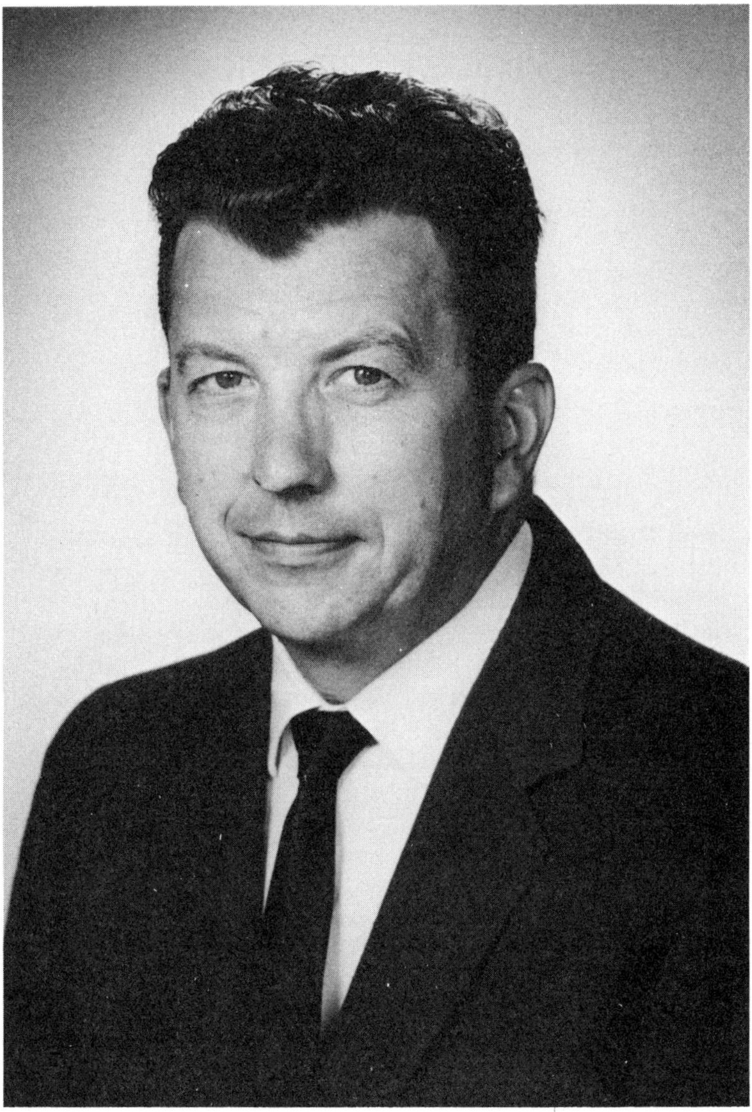

Mrs. DOZIER

Meet Mrs. DOZIER. A staff nurse, Mrs. DOZIER must keep copious records (DOSSIERS, that is) on many patients. So picture Mrs. Dozier with a stack of DOSSIERS, and tie it in with the outstanding physical feature. You might want to turn the tables on Nurse DOZIER and give her a DOSE of HER own medicine. There are several nice features to remember Mrs. DOZIER by.

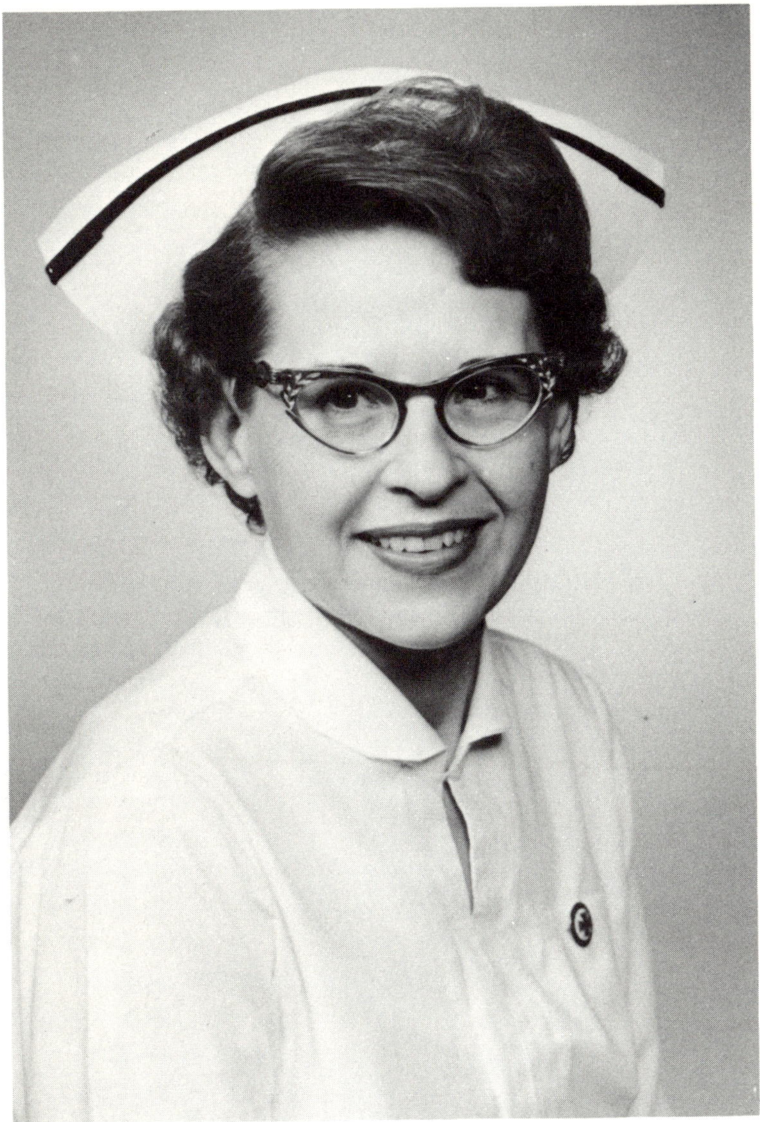

Mr. JARL

Meet Mr. JARL. It's an uncommon name, but try this gimmick: visualize an ordinary JAR; now simply add an L to it. Result, of course, is JARL. For good measure, recall that JARL, an erstwhile athlete, could easily JAR you. Again, remember that JAR plus L equals JARL.

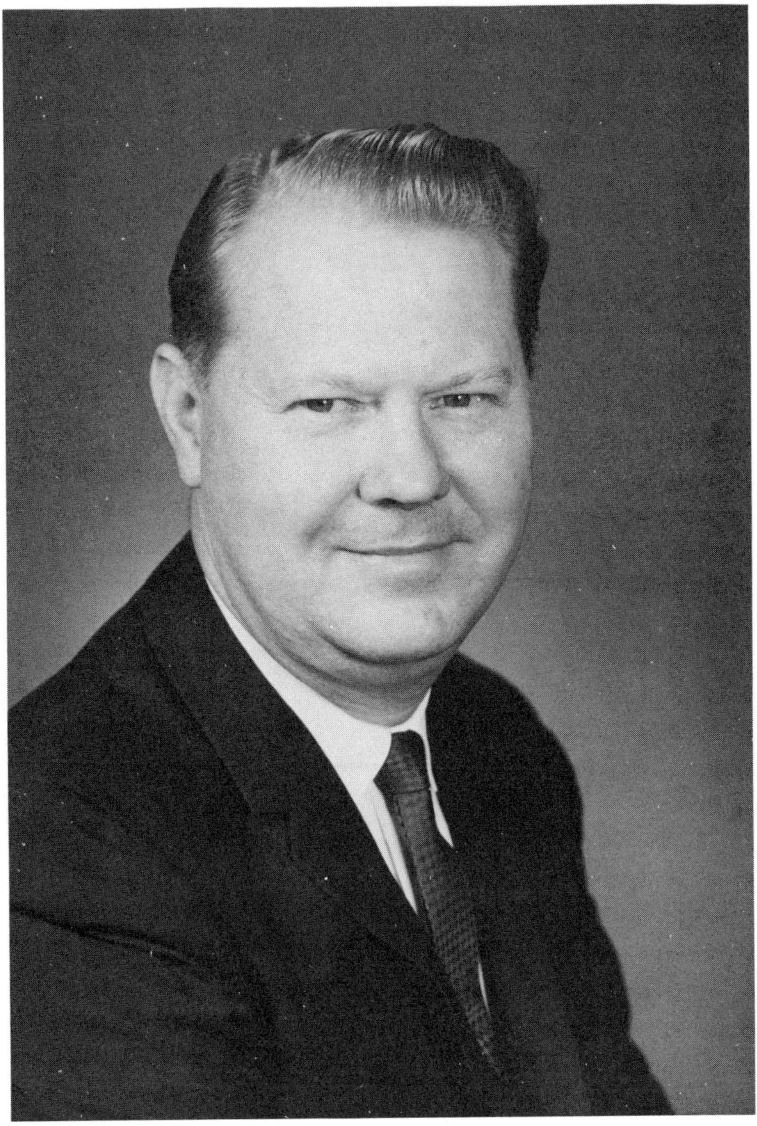

Peggy HEAD

Meet Peggy HEAD. "Well-bred, well-read—that's our Peggy HEAD." A memorable, if not classic jingle. Using her attractive HEAD as a physical tag, it's surely not difficult to visualize Peggy HEAD getting a-HEAD. Remember Peggy, and you'll go to the HEAD of the class.

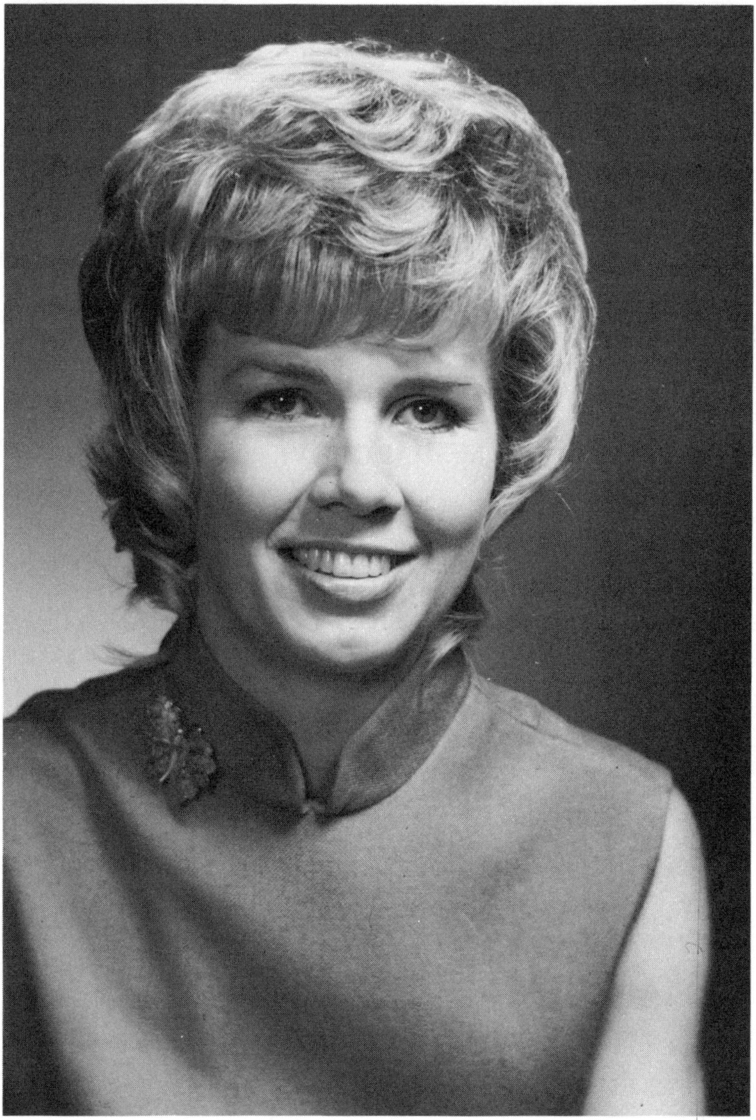

Mr. HARGROVE

Meet Mr. HARGROVE, who has the same name as a famed World War II yardbird, Private HARGROVE. Pick out any one of Mr. HARGROVE's several nice features and visualize Private HARGROVE typing away on his best-selling book. Maybe you'd like to select the slightly receding hairline and think of it as a HAIR-GROOVE. But remember, it's: "See here, Mr. HARGROVE."

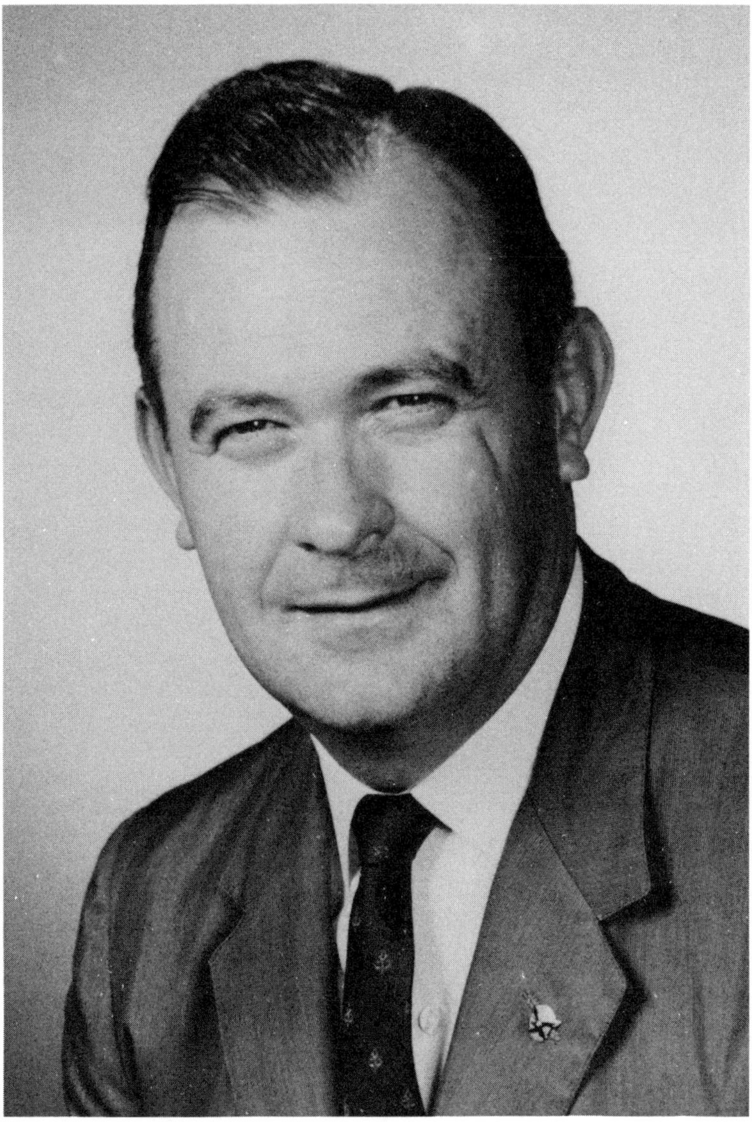

Carol LAMIA

Meet Carol LAMIA. Pronounced LAMB-ee-uh, which means that phonetically, the key word to remember is LAMB. It shouldn't be too difficult, then, to recall that Carol is "as gentle as a LAMB-ee-uh." She has several nice features for easy identification. A top-notch executive secretary, she'll never take it on the LAMB-ee-uh.

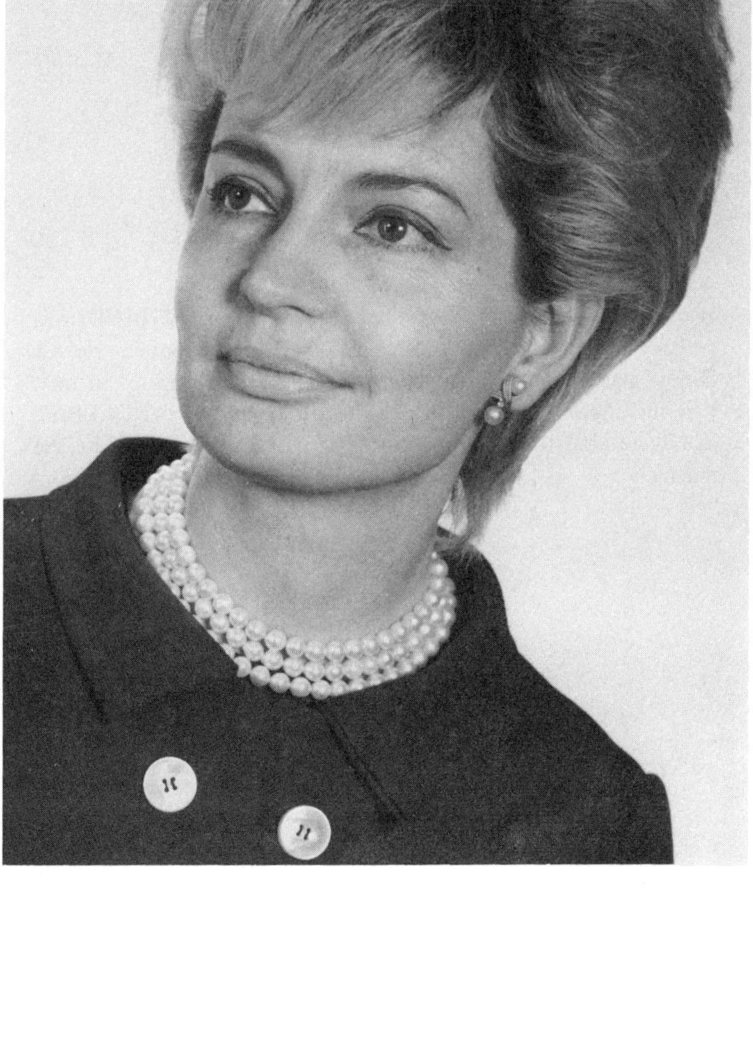

Mr. CHANDLER

Meet Mr. CHANDLER. Visualize him with another CHANDLER, perhaps "Happy" Chandler, ex-baseball commissioner. He's a family man, but could readily pass as a real "swinger." In fact, you just might visualize him swinging from a CHANDELIER. You'll be able to identify Mr. CHANDLER quite easily by the mustache.

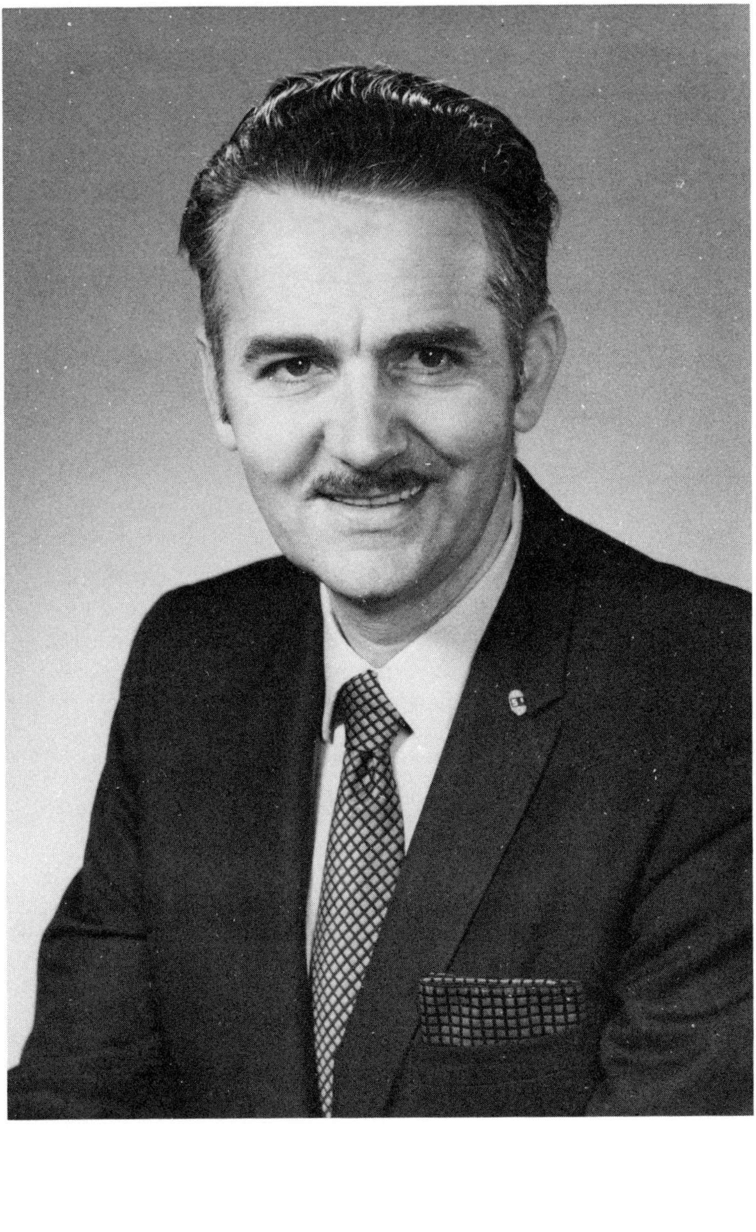

Mary SINGER

Meet Mary SINGER. Though Mrs. SINGER isn't a professional vocalist, she still passes as quite a SINGER. You might even say she's a merry SINGER. Another SINGER comes to mind—that of sewing-machine fame. It's appropriate because she's the mother of four. Visualize a merry tune coming from Mary SINGER.

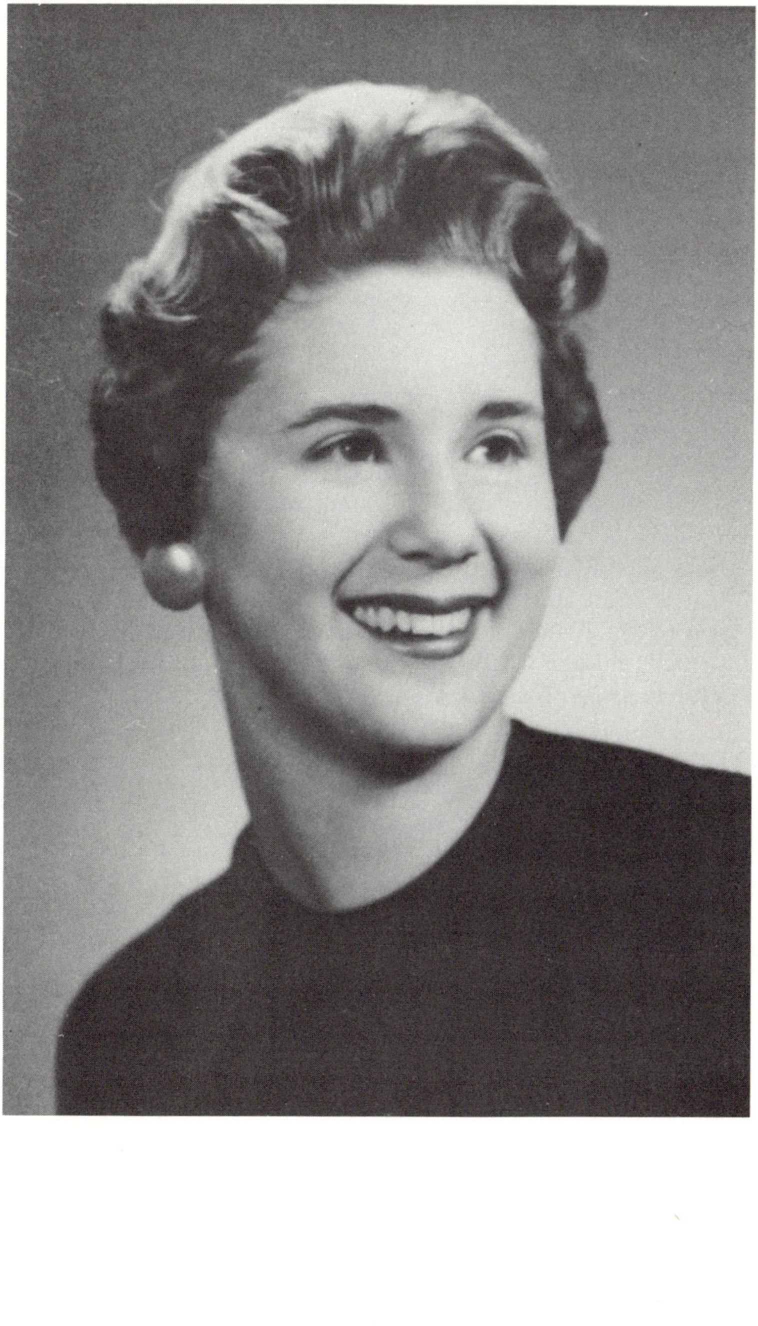

Mr. CROW

Meet Mr. CROW, who has a fine head of hair. So fine, in fact, that it might make a good CROW's nest. So visualize a CROW's nest (either a bird's or a ship's) atop Mr. CROW's hair. Also note the faint trace of CROW's feet near Mr. CROW's handsome eyes when he smiles. That's Mr. CROW.

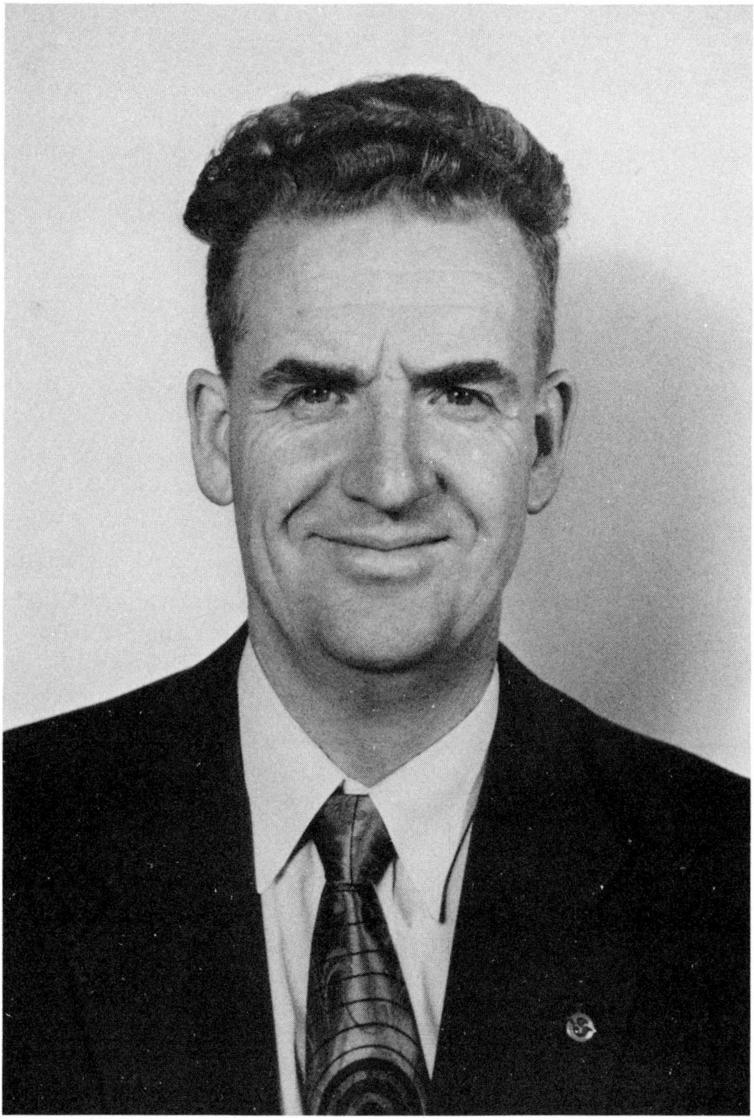

Mr. JUSTICE

Meet Mr. JUSTICE. As a police reporter, Mr. JUSTICE was quite interested in JUSTICE. Later, as a prize-winning science writer, Mr. JUSTICE covered the scientific waterfront. This included junkets to places like Antarctica, which was JUST-ICE as far as Mr. JUSTICE was concerned. You might want to remember him as "JUSTICE of the the press." Remember, Mr. JUSTICE.

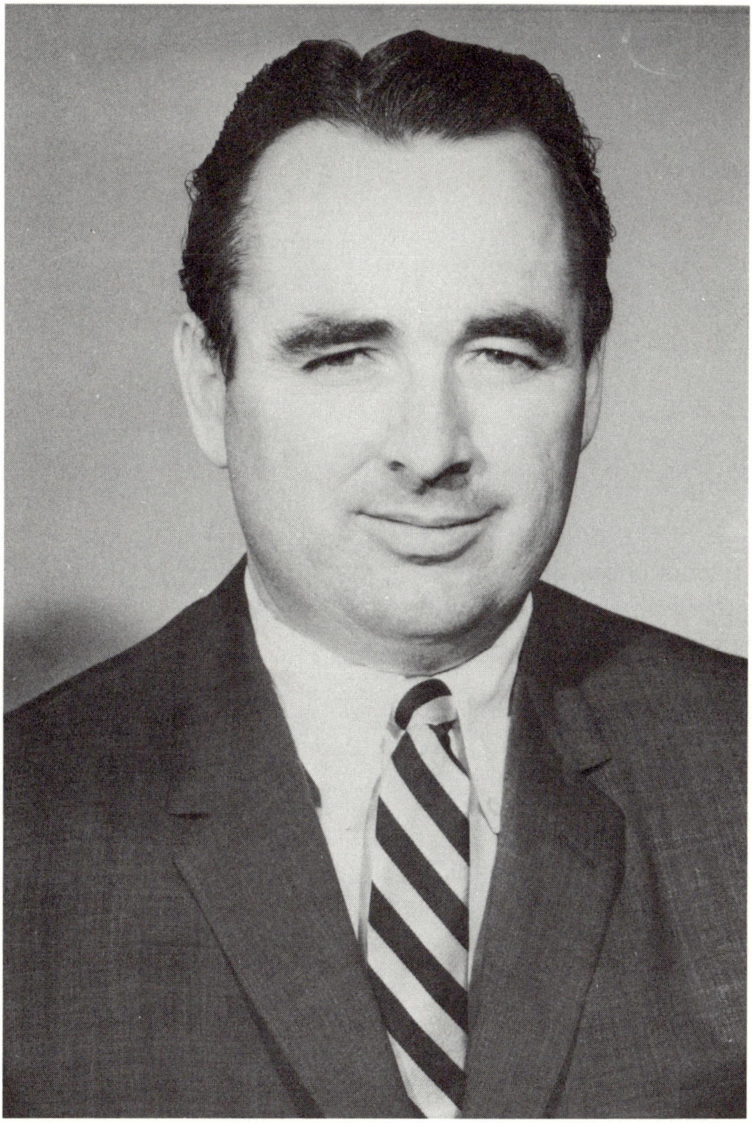

Introductions are complete. Now take a brief break, then look at the following pages and see if you can identify the people whom you just met.

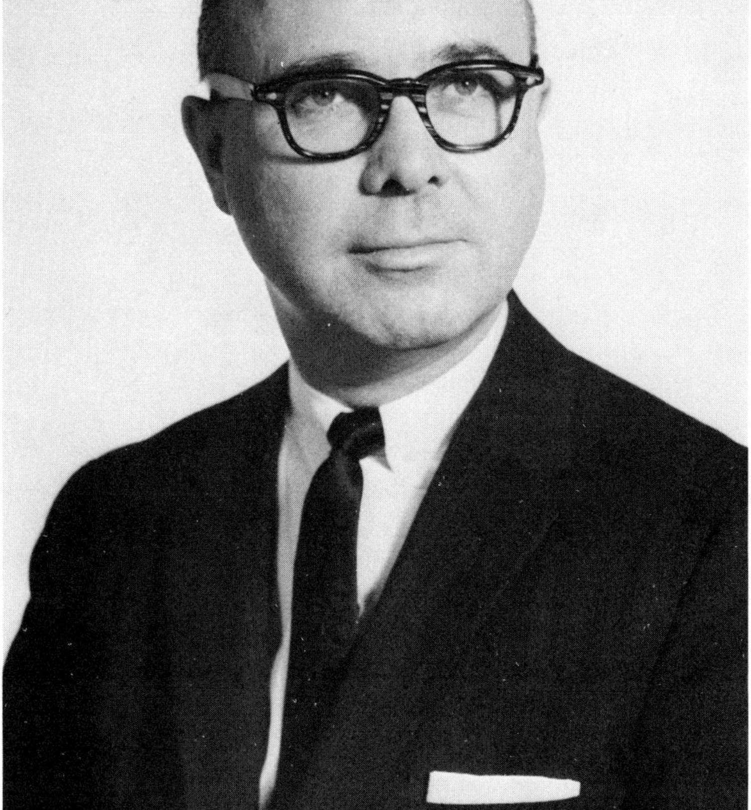

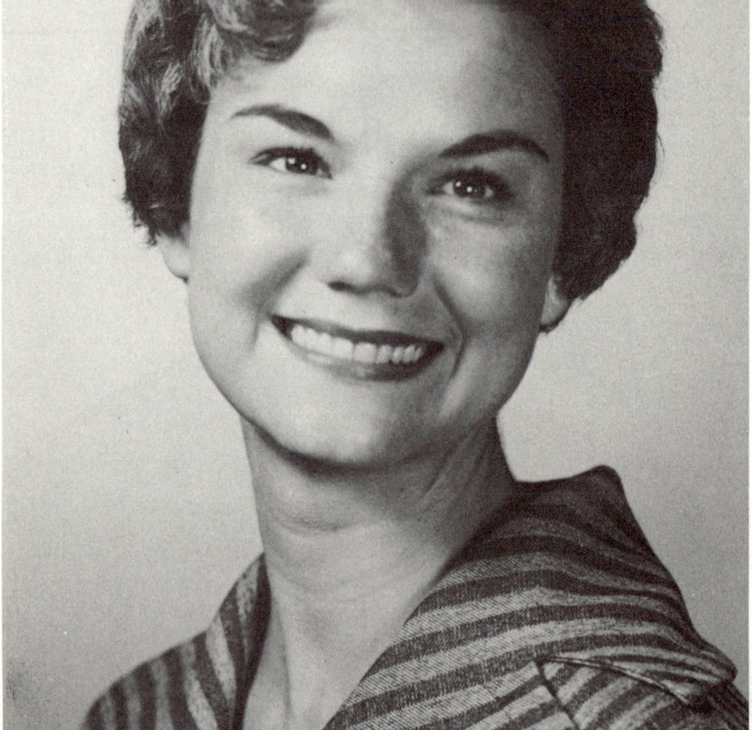

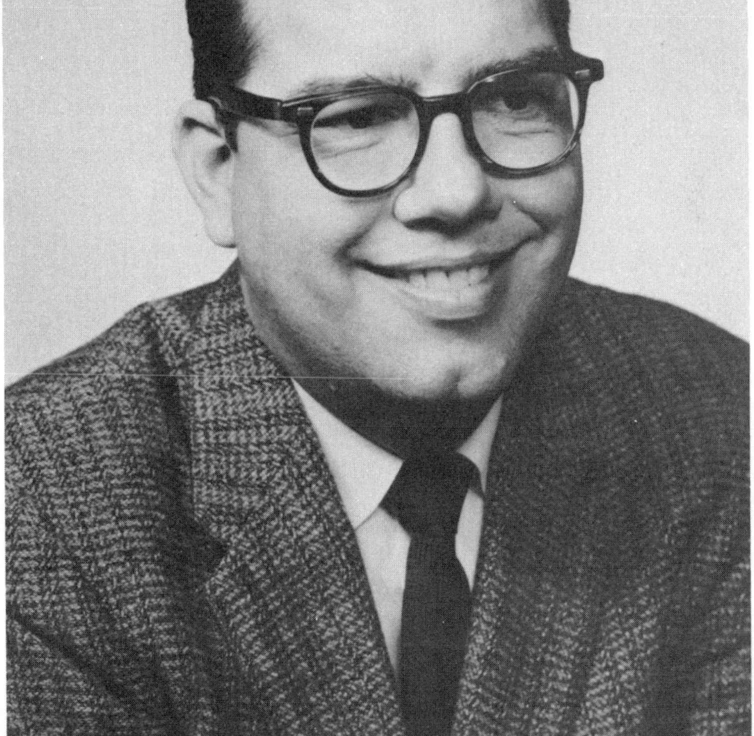

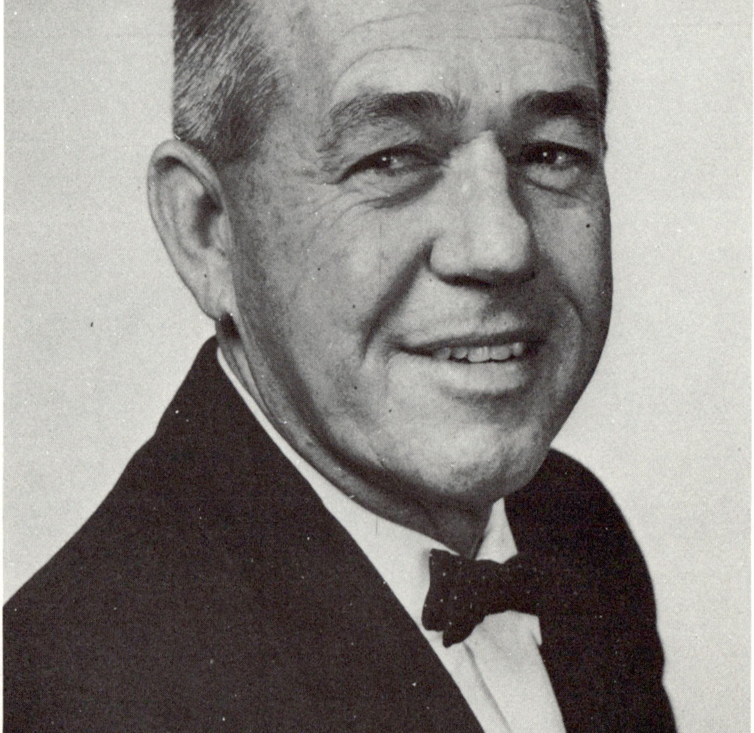

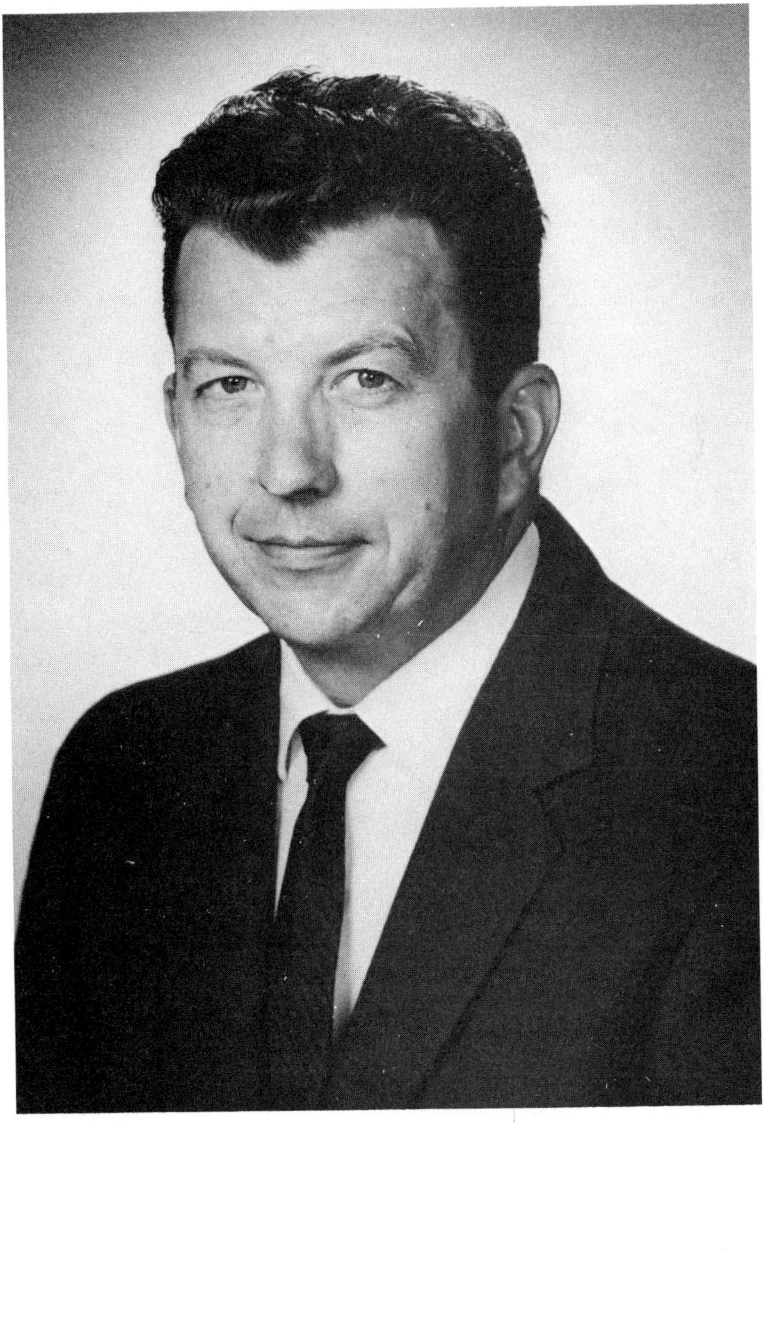

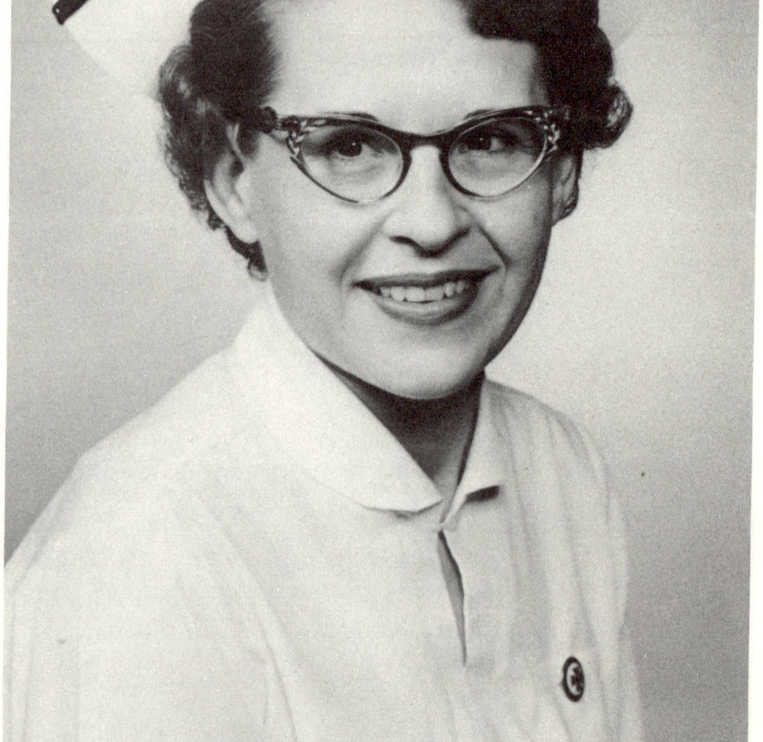

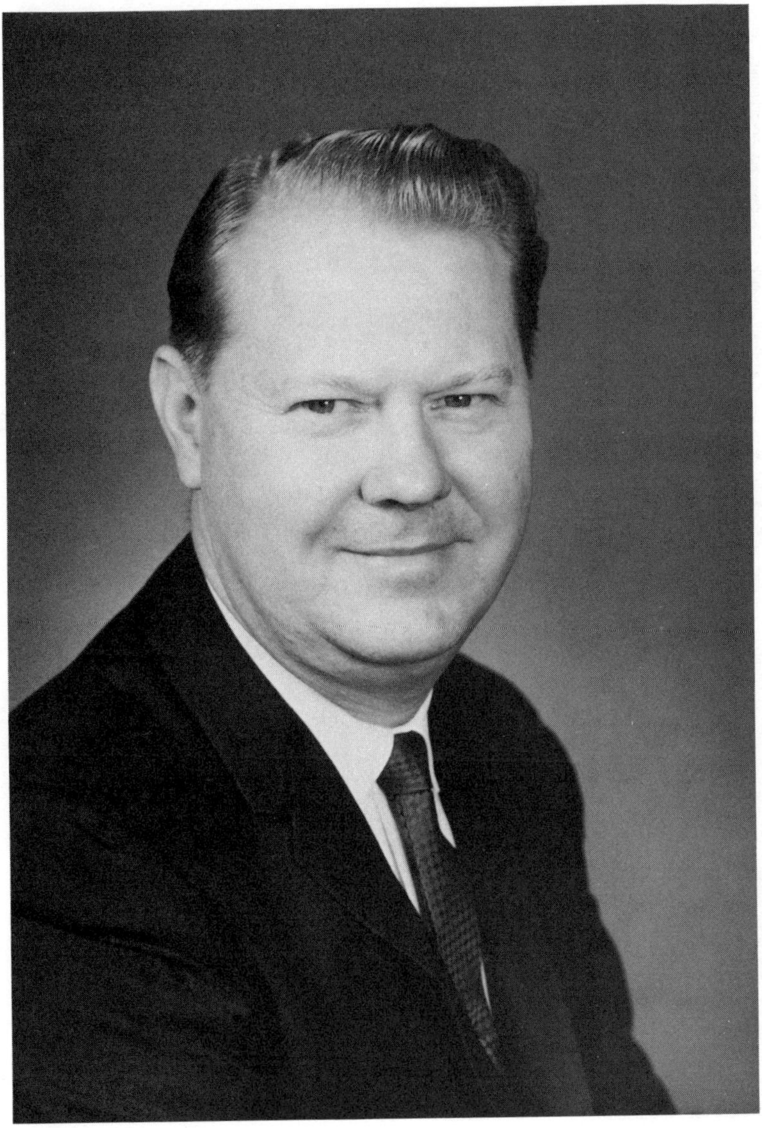

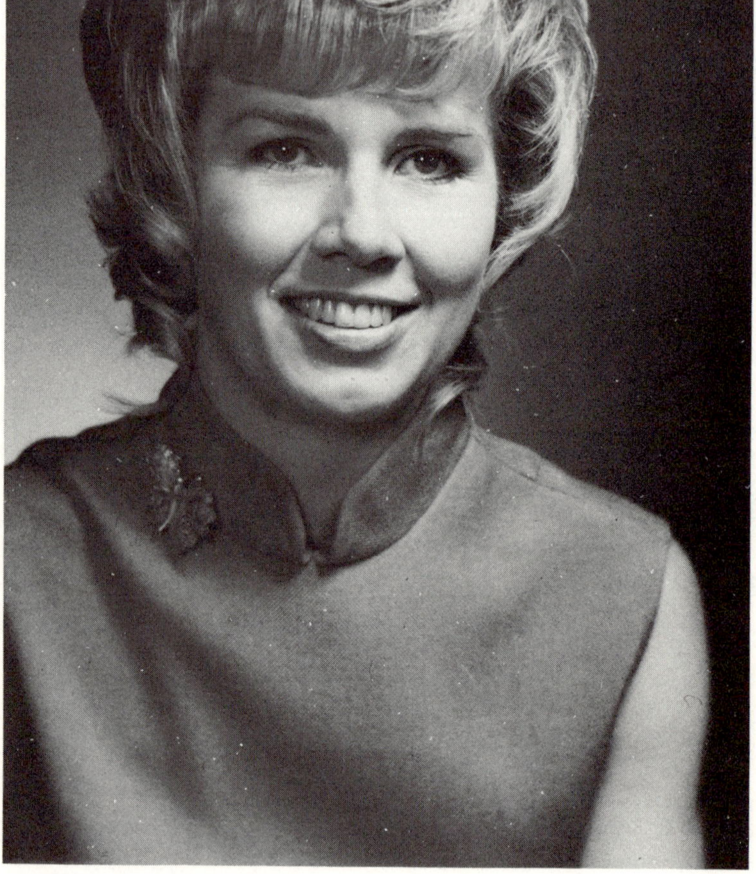

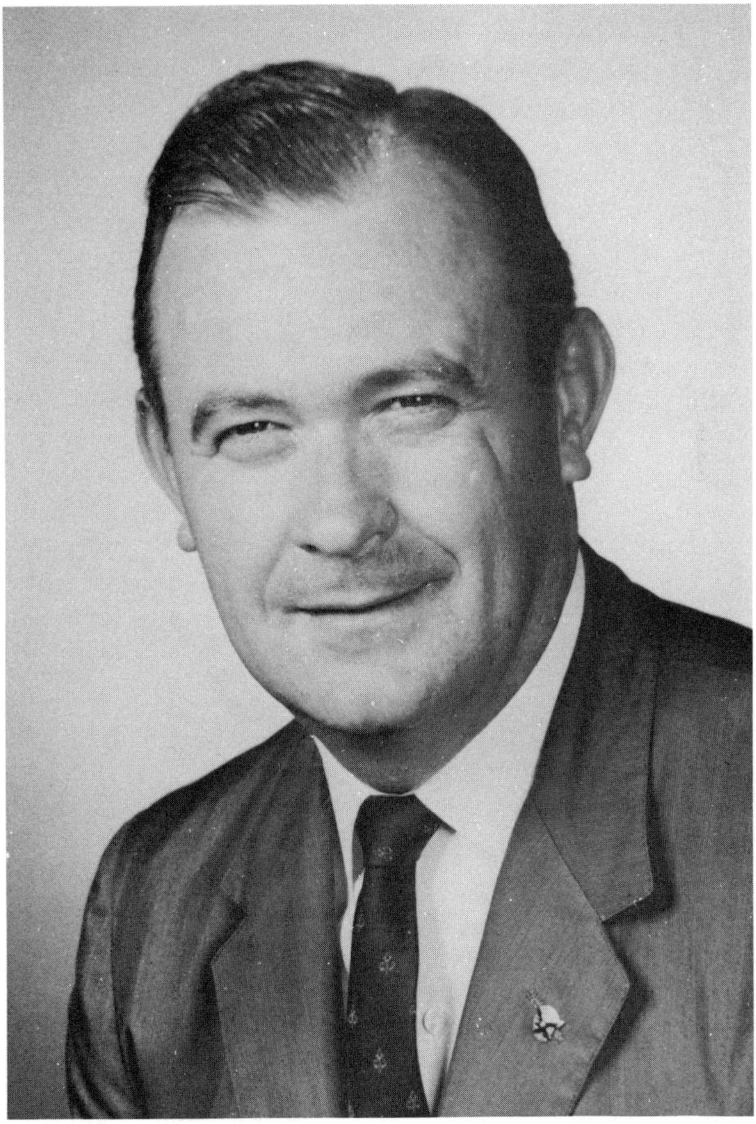

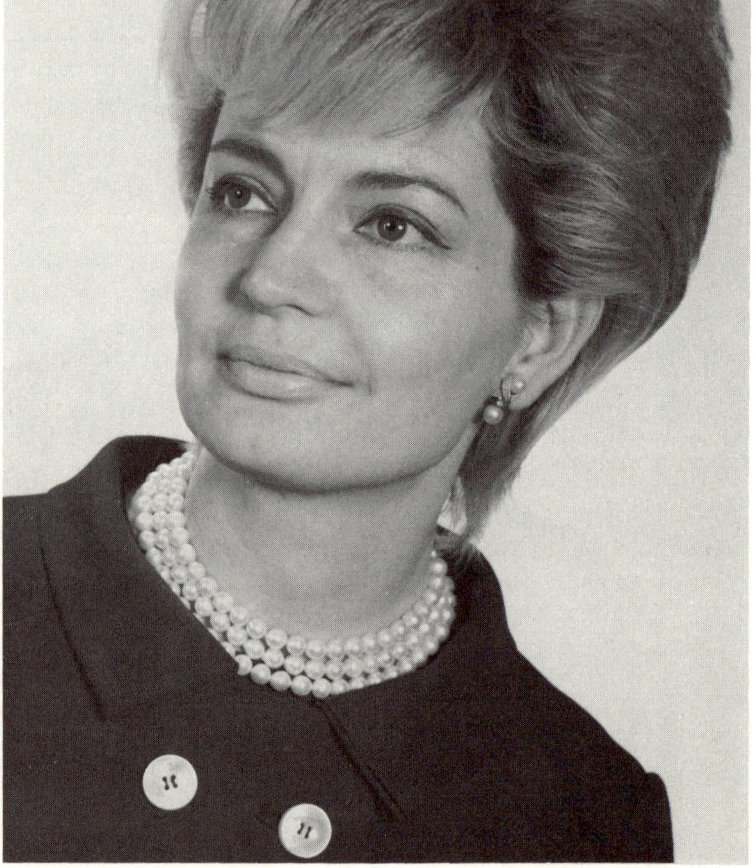

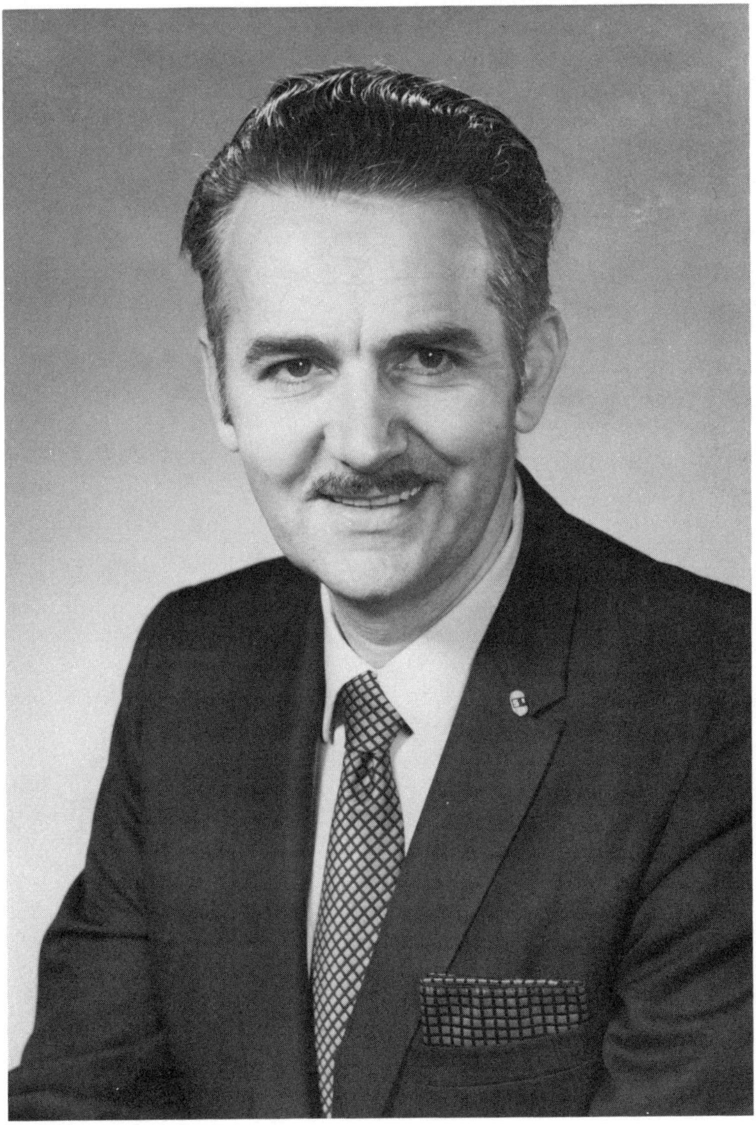

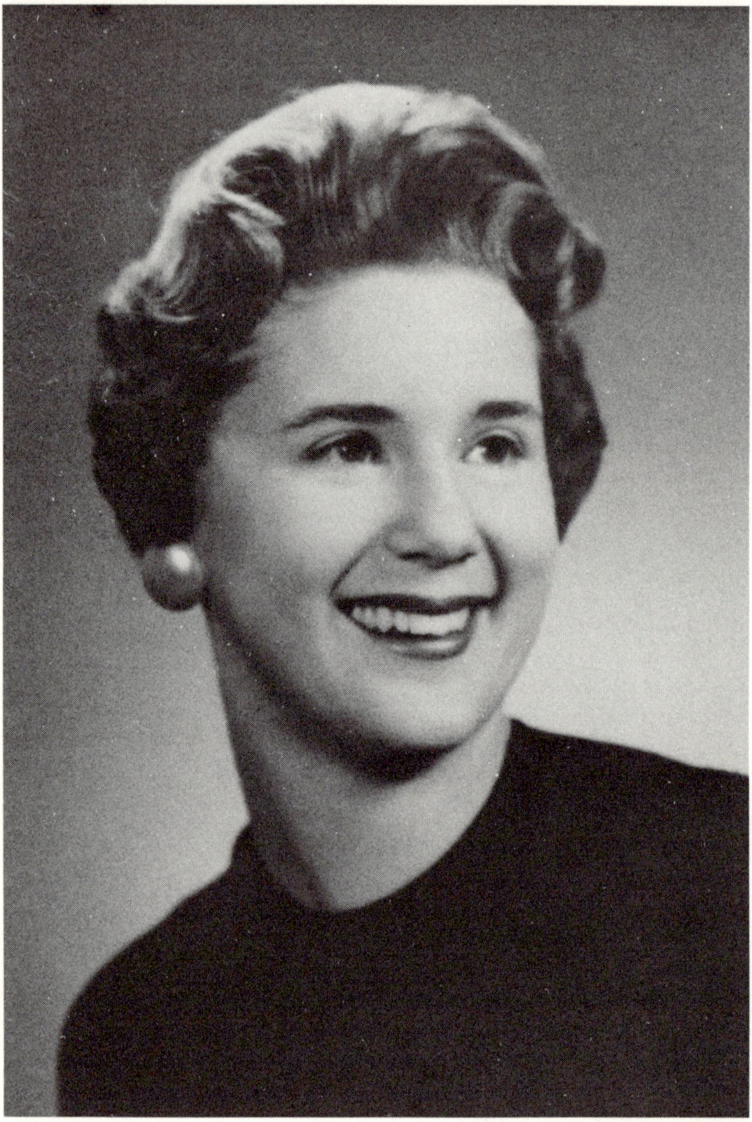

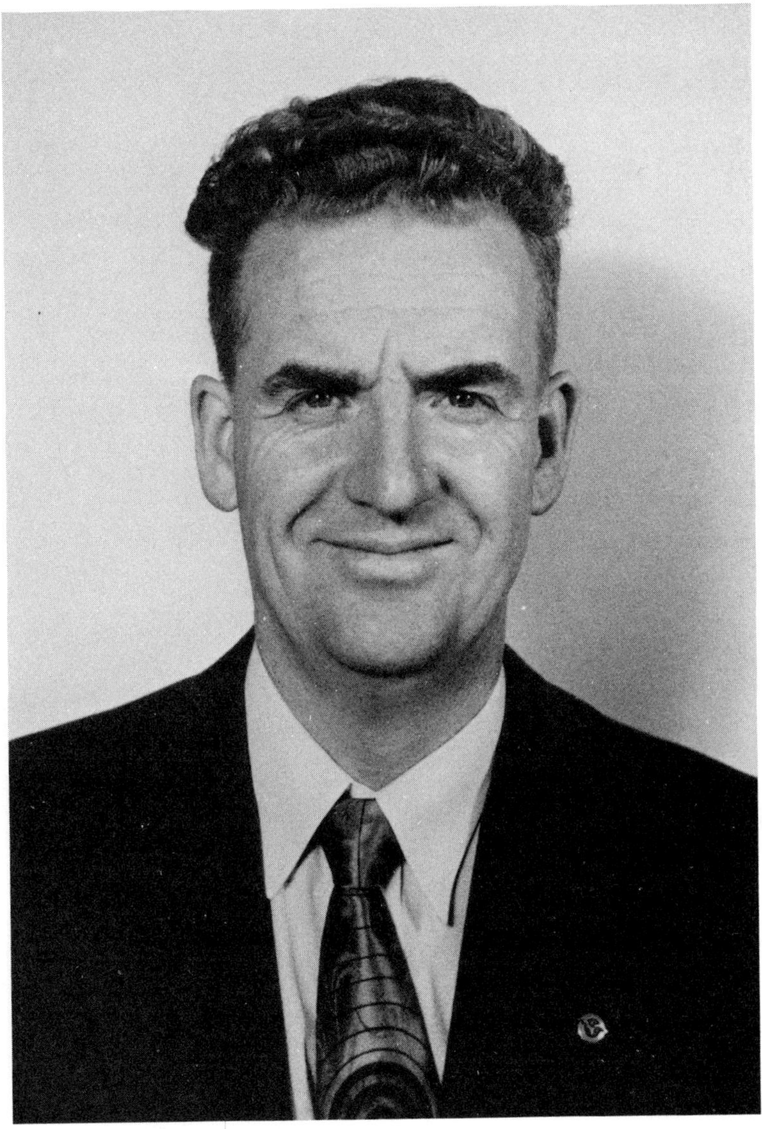

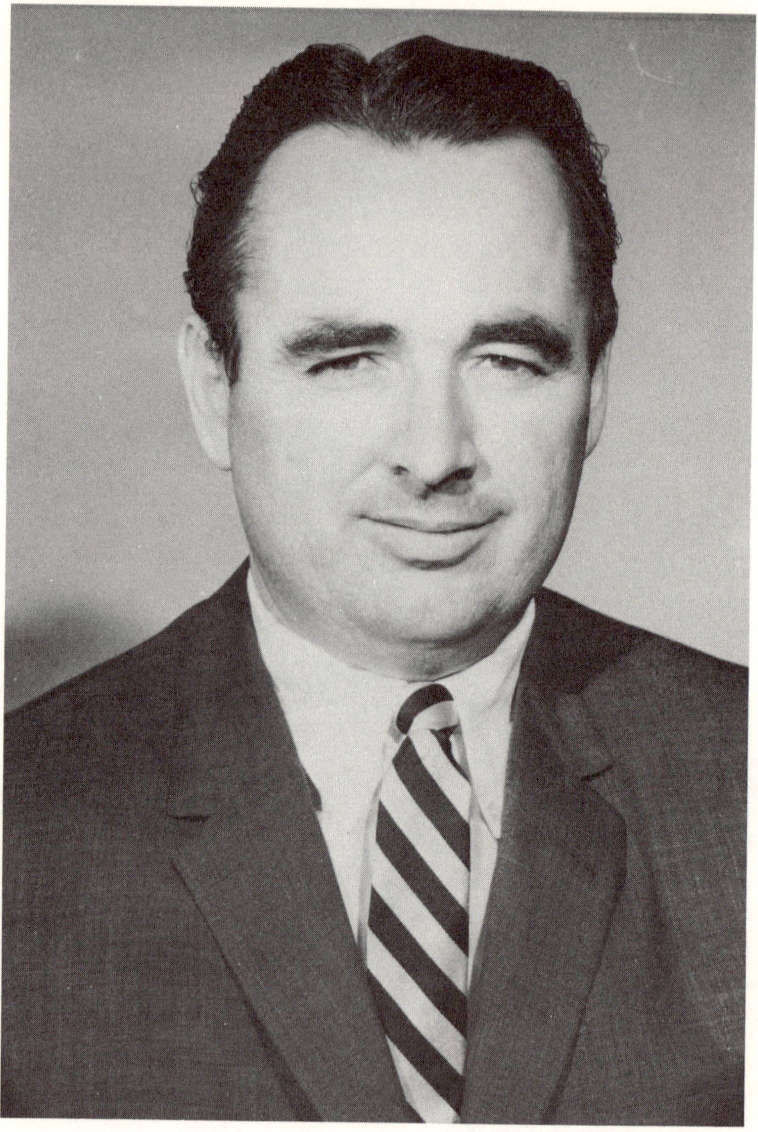

How did you do? If you got 11 or more correct, you could be on your way to becoming an instant name-rememberer.

If you didn't do too well, don't despair. With a little more practice, you can still get excellent results.

Review the names you missed. Try to pinpoint your weakness. Maybe you weren't concentrating. Possibly you didn't visualize the outstanding feature or make a vivid association. Maybe you should have made more than one association.

One note of caution. Even though you got all the names correct, it's prudent to question whether you have really *mastered* them. Are they etched "permanently" in your memory?

They probably are *not,* for a couple of good reasons: first, you learned the names only as an exercise and probably didn't *intend* to remember them over a long period of time; second, most of the associations you made must be regarded as somewhat tentative until they have passed the test of time. Can you recall the name next week, next month, next year?

Realizing this, people like H.B. Upton, vice-president of the First National Bank of Tahlequah in Cherokee County, Oklahoma, prefer to keep a "memory file" on names.

Upton has a reputation for being able to call by name virtually any customer who walks into his bank.

Starting Your Name Notebook

He, like others who can perform similar feats, is able to do so because he is genuinely interested in people, and makes mental—and written—notes about them during the introduction.

During or shortly after the introduction, he'll write down facts about the person in a 3-by-5 notebook. Later, he'll record the information in a permanent name file.

Information to be written down might include such things as name, approximate age, address (usually city), physical description (including outstanding feature), hobbies, and miscellaneous relevant information about the person.

Why not experiment with this technique, which has worked so well for Mr. Upton and others who are genuinely interested in

200 Using Instant Memory Power to Remember Names—Shortcut to Success

remembering customers' names? Copy the form below in a pocket-size notebook ten times. Make notes on the next ten people you meet. You might want to change the format to suit your needs better. If the technique works for you, you can start making notes regularly.

Name _____ Nickname _____

Address _____

Age _____ Build _____ Color eyes _____

Outstanding feature _____

Miscellaneous _____

Remember, you're trying a new technique—a technique that takes some time and plenty of practice to master. You should practice every day. If you stay with it, chances are you'll soon be amazing yourself and your friends with your ability to recall names. This is surely the acid test for the person who would develop instant memory power.